Collins

Year 7, Pupil Book 1

NEW MATHS FRAMEWORKING

Matches the revised KS3 Framework

Kevin Evans, Keith Gordon, Trevor Senior, Brian Speed

William Collins' dream of knowledge for all began with the publication of his first book in 1819. A self-educated mill worker, he not only enriched millions of lives, but also founded a flourishing publishing house. Today, staying true to this spirit, Collins books are packed with inspiration, innovation and practical expertise. They place you at the centre of a world of possibility and give you exactly what you need to explore it.

Collins. Freedom to teach.

Published by Collins
An imprint of HarperCollins*Publishers*
77–85 Fulham Palace Road
Hammersmith
London
W6 8JB

Browse the complete Collins catalogue at
www.collinseducation.com

ISBN 978-0-00-726608-1

Keith Gordon, Kevin Evans, Brian Speed and Trevor Senior assert their moral rights to be identified as the authors of this work.

British Library Cataloguing in Publication Data
A Catalogue record for this publication is available from the British Library.

Commissioned by Melanie Hoffman and Katie Sergeant
Project management by Priya Govindan
Edited by Brian Ashbury
Proofread by Amanda Dickson
Indexed by Michael Forder
Design and typesetting by Jordan Publishing Design
Covers by Oculus Design and Communications
Functional maths spreads and covers management by Laura Deacon
Illustrations by Nigel Jordan and Tony Wilkins
Printed and bound by Printing Express, Hong Kong
Production by Simon Moore

Acknowledgments
The publishers thank the Qualifications and Curriculum Authority for granting permission to reproduce questions from past National Curriculum Test papers for Key Stage 3 Maths.

The publishers wish to thank the following for permission to reproduce photographs:

p.24–25 (main image) © Jon Hicks / Corbis, p.56–57 (main image) © Van Hilversum / Alamy, p.56 (football image) © istockphoto.com, p.84–85 (main image) © istockphoto.com, p.84 (inset image) © istockphoto.com, p.96–97 (main image) © Ted Levine / zefa / Corbis, p.96–97 (inset images) © istockphoto.com, p.116–117 (main image) © Jeff Morgan food and drink / Alamy, p. 116–117 (all inset images) © istockphoto.com, p.132–133 (main image) © Science Photo Library, p. 132–133 (all inset images) © istockphoto.com, p.162–163 (main image) © Stephen Vowles / Alamy, p.170–171 (main image) © Sean Justice / Corbis, p.184–185 (all images) © istockphoto.com, p.204–205 (main and inset images) © istockphoto.com

Every effort has been made to trace copyright holders and to obtain their permission for the use of copyright material. The authors and publishers will gladly receive any information enabling them to rectify any error or omission at the first opportunity.

Mixed Sources
Product group from well-managed forests and other controlled sources
www.fsc.org Cert no. SW-COC-1806
© 1996 Forest Stewardship Council

FSC is a non-profit international organisation established to promote the responsible management of the world's forests. Products carrying the FSC label are independently certified to assure consumers that they come from forests that are managed to meet the social, economic and ecological needs of present and future generations.

Find out more about HarperCollins and the environment at
www.harpercollins.co.uk/green

Contents

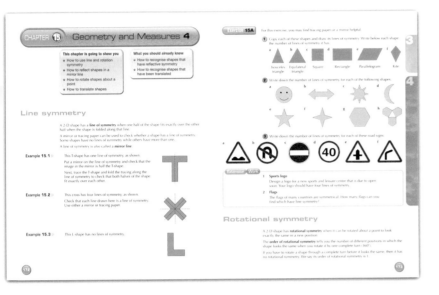

Learning objectives

See what you are going to cover and what you should already know at the start of each chapter. The purple and blue boxes set the topic in context and provide a handy checklist.

National Curriculum levels

Know what level you are working at so you can easily track your progress with the colour-coded levels at the side of the page.

Worked examples

Understand the topic before you start the exercises by reading the examples in blue boxes. These take you through how to answer a question step-by-step.

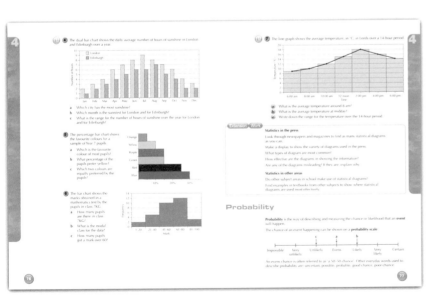

Functional Maths

Practise your Functional Maths skills to see how people use Maths in everyday life.

 Look out for the Functional Maths icon on the page.

Extension activities

Stretch your thinking and investigative skills by working through the extension activities. By tackling these you are working at a higher level.

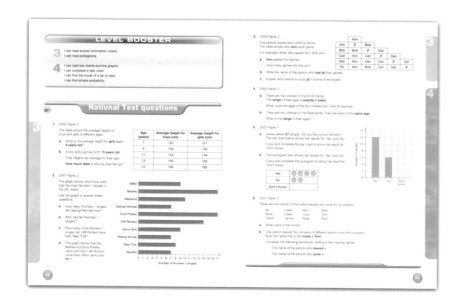

Level booster

Progress to the next level by checking the Level boosters at the end of each chapter. These clearly show you what you need to know at each level and how to improve.

National Test questions

Practise the past paper Test questions to feel confident and prepared for your KS3 National Curriculum Tests. The questions are levelled so you can check what level you are working at.

Extra interactive National Test practice

Watch and listen to the audio/visual National Test questions on the separate Interactive Book CD-ROM to help you revise as a class on a whiteboard.

 Look out for the computer mouse icon on the page and on the screen.

Functional Maths activities

Put Maths into context with these colourful pages showing real-world situations involving Maths. You are practising your Functional Maths skills by analysing data to solve problems.

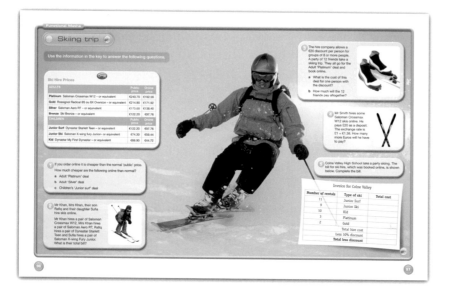

Extra interactive Functional Maths questions and video clips

Extend your Functional Maths skills by taking part in the interactive questions on the separate Interactive Book CD-ROM. Your teacher can put these on the whiteboard so the class can answer the questions on the board.

See Maths in action by watching the video clips and doing the related Worksheets on the Interactive Book CD-ROM. The videos bring the Functional Maths activities to life and help you see how Maths is used in the real world.

 Look out for the computer mouse icon on the page and on the screen.

<table>
<tr><td>

This chapter is going to show you

- How to read timetables and calendars
- How to work out the interval between two times on, for example, a bus timetable
- How to convert between the 24- and 12-hour clocks

</td><td>

What you should already know

- How to tell the time using a regular and a digital clock
- The names of the months
- The names of the days in a week

</td></tr>
</table>

The calendar

Time is based on the movement of the planets around the Sun and the rotation of the Earth. This is why there are 365 days in a year (or 366 every four years, which is called a leap year). Each year is divided into 12 months and approximately 52 weeks. Each week is 7 days. Each day is 24 hours and each hour is 60 minutes. Each minute is 60 seconds.

Because nothing quite divides evenly, the same dates each year will fall on different days.

Due to historical reasons, the twelve months which make up the year do not have the same number of days. Most months have 31 days. Four months – April, June, September and November – have 30 days, and February has 28 days in most years or 29 days every leap year.

Example 1.1

The calendar shows January, February, March and April for 2008.

January 2008

M	T	W	T	F	S	S
	1	2	3	4	5	6
7	8	9	10	11	12	13
14	15	16	17	18	19	20
21	22	23	24	25	26	27
28	29	30	31			

February 2008

M	T	W	T	F	S	S
				1	2	3
4	5	6	7	8	9	10
11	12	13	14	15	16	17
18	19	20	21	22	23	24
25	26	27	28	29		

March 2008

M	T	W	T	F	S	S
					1	2
3	4	5	6	7	8	9
10	11	12	13	14	15	16
17	18	19	20	21	22	23
24	25	26	27	28	29	30
31						

April 2008

M	T	W	T	F	S	S
	1	2	3	4	5	6
7	8	9	10	11	12	13
14	15	16	17	18	19	20
21	22	23	24	25	26	27
28	29	30				

a How do you know that 2008 is a leap year?

b Which two months have five Wednesdays in them?

c Mr Patel goes on a skiing holiday. He arrives at the resort on Friday 25th January and leaves on Sunday 3rd February. How many nights does he stay at the resort?

d Mr Brown is a teacher. He returns to work on Wednesday the 2nd of January after Christmas. He has a half-term holiday from 9th February to 17th February. The first day of the Easter holiday is 21st March. How many days does he work in the Spring term?

e Mrs Khan's birthday is on 7th May. What day of the week will this be?

Example 1.1

continued

a Because February has 29 days, it must be a leap year.

b Looking down the Wednesday column, you can see that January and April both have five Wednesdays in them.

c Count the days from the 25th to the 2nd (his last night). He stays for 9 nights.

d He works 22 days in January, 16 days in February and 14 days in March. 22 + 16 + 14 = 52 days.

e The 1st of May is Thursday so count on to the 7th. This is on a Wednesday.

Exercise 1A

1 How many days are there in:

   a 3 weeks?   b 12 weeks?   c 52 weeks?

2 How many hours are there in:

   a 4 days?   b a week?   c July?

3 How many minutes are there in:

   a 2 hours?   b $5\frac{1}{2}$ hours?   c a day?

4 How many seconds are there in:

   a 5 minutes?   b 24 minutes?   c one hour?

5 How many minutes are there in:

   a 120 seconds?   b 300 seconds?

6 How many hours and minutes are there in:

   a 200 minutes?   b 350 minutes?

7 2008 is a leap year. When is the next leap year?

8 How many days are in June, July and August together?

9 Judy was born on 5th August 1996. Punch was born on 6th September 1996. How many days older than Punch is Judy?

FM 10 The calendar shows June, July and August of 2008. Saturday the 12th of July is circled.

June 2008

M	T	W	T	F	S	S
						1
2	3	4	5	6	7	8
9	10	11	12	13	14	15
16	17	18	19	20	21	22
23	24	25	26	27	28	29
30						

July 2008

M	T	W	T	F	S	S
	1	2	3	4	5	6
7	8	9	10	11	12	13
14	15	16	17	18	19	20
21	22	23	24	25	26	27
28	29	30	31			

August 2008

M	T	W	T	F	S	S
				1	2	3
4	5	6	7	8	9	10
11	12	13	14	15	16	17
18	19	20	21	22	23	24
25	26	27	28	29	30	31

a What day of the week is the 8th of July?

(b) What date is the 3rd Saturday in August?

(c) The Marley family flew to Florida on the 4th of August and flew back on the 18th August. How many nights were they in Florida?

(d) Mr Green has a physiotherapy appointment every two weeks. His last appointment was on 29th May. What date is his next appointment?

(e) The first day of the school holidays is Thursday the 24th of July. The first day back at school is Wednesday the 3rd of September. How many days do the school holidays last?

Extension **Work**

How to work out the day you were born on.

Take the date (say, 5th August 1998).

Step 1: Take the last 2 digits of the year, multiply by 1.25 and ignore any decimals.

$$98 \times 1.25 = 122.5 = 122$$

Step 2: Add the day.

$$122 + 5 = 127$$

Step 3: Add 0 for May, 1 for August, 2 for February, March or November, 3 for June, 4 for September or December, 5 for April or July, 6 for January or October.

$$127 + 1 = 128$$

Step 4: If the date is in the 1900s, add 1.

$$128 + 1 = 129$$

Step 5: If the year is a leap year and the month is January or February, subtract 1.

1998 is not a leap year.

Step 6: Divide by 7 and get the remainder.

$$129 \div 7 = 18 \text{ remainder } 3$$

Step 7: The remainder tells you the day.

0 = Sunday, 1 = Monday, 2 = Tuesday, 3 = Wednesday, 4 = Thursday, 5 = Friday, 6 = Saturday

So the 5th of August 1998 was a Wednesday.

You can check by doing a Google search for 'Calendar 1998'.

Work out the day for your Birthday or a friend's birthday.

The 12-hour and 24-hour clock

There are two types of clock: the normal type, which looks like this, is called an analogue clock and tells the time using the 12-hour clock system.

The other type are called digital clocks and have displays like this:

Digital clocks can tell the time using both the 12-hour and 24-hour clock system. Afternoon times in the 24-hour clock are found by adding twelve onto the 12-hour clock time, so 4:30 pm is 1630h. The 'h' stands for hours and the time is often read as 'sixteen thirty hours'.

Most timetables and television schedules use the 24-hour clock.

Example 1.2

The four clocks below show the time that Jamil gets up (clock A), has lunch (clock B), finishes work (clock C) and goes to bed (clock D).

a Fill in the table to show the time of each clock using the 12-hour and 24-hour clock.

Clock	A	B	C	D
12-hour	6:30 am			11:00 pm
24-hour		1245	1715	

b How long is there between Jamil getting up and going to bed?

c If Jamil starts work at 8:30 and takes an hour for lunch, how many hours is he at work?

a 6:30 am is 0630 hours, 1245 hours is 12:45 pm, 1715 hours is 5:15 pm and 11:00 pm is 2300 hours.

b Jamil gets up at 0630 hours and goes to bed at 2300 hours. To work out the difference, use a time line:

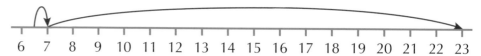

From 0630 to 0700 is 30 minutes. From 0700 to 2300 is 16 hours.

The answer is 16 hours and 30 minutes.

c 0830 to 0900 is 30 minutes, 0900 to 1700 is 8 hours and 1700 to 1715 is 15 minutes.

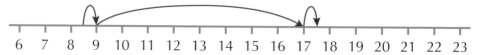

Total time is 8 hours plus 30 minutes plus 15 minutes less 1 hour for lunch = 7 hours and 45 minutes.

Time on a calculator: Because there are only 60 minutes in an hour, it is not possible to type values directly into a calculator. The following table shows the decimal equivalent of some times in minutes:

Minutes	6 mins	15 mins	20 mins	30 mins	40 mins	45 mins
Decimal	0.1	0.25	0.33	0.5	0.67	0.75

Example 1.3

Write the following times as decimals:

a 4h 30m   **b** 2h 40m   **c** 1h 36m

a Using the table above, 4h 30m = 4.5 h

b 2h 40m = 2.67 h

c As 6 minutes is 0.1 hours, 36m = 6 × 6 = 6 × 0.1 = 0.6 h, so 1h 36m = 1.6 h

Timetables:

Whenever we travel on a bus or train, we need to read a timetable to find out the times that the bus or train leaves and arrives at its destination.

Example 1.4

The following timetable shows the train times from Sheffield to Huddersfield via Barnsley:

Sheffield	0536	0642	0745	0845	0955	1106	1213
Barnsley	0601	↓	0813	0913	↓	1132	1247
Penistone	0618	↓	0839	0939	↓	1200	1310
Huddersfield	0648	0738	0910	1010	1051	1230	1338

a How long does the 0536 take to get from Sheffield to Huddersfield?

b The 0642 is a direct train. What do the symbols ↓ mean?

c Mary arrives at Barnsley station at 1120. How long does she have to wait for the next train to Huddersfield?

d Jamil has to be in Penistone for a meeting at 10 am. What time train should he catch from Sheffield?

a 1 hour after 0536 is 0636. The train gets to Huddersfield at 0648 which is 12 minutes later than 0636. So the train takes 1 hour and 12 minutes.

b The symbol means that the train d does not stop at these stations.

c The next train is at 1132, so she has to wait for 12 minutes.

d To be in Penistone for 10 am, he needs to arrive on the 0939, which leaves Sheffield at 0845.

Exercise 1B

1 Write these 12-hour clock times in the 24-hour clock.

a	5 am	**b**	5 pm	**c**	11:20 am
d	5:15 pm	**e**	11:05 pm	**f**	10:05 am

2 Write these 24-hour clock times as 12-hour clock times using am and pm.

a	1800	**b**	0700	**c**	1215
d	1620	**e**	2230	**f**	1107

3 How many hours and minutes are there between the following times?

a	0930 to 1330	**b**	0815 to 1045
c	1820 to 2230	**d**	0622 to 0933
e	0645 to 1530	**f**	1112 to 2328

 4 A TV programme starts at 1750 and finishes at 1825. How long is the programme?

 5 A TV programme starts at 9:55 and is 25 minutes long. At what time does it finish?

6 Copy and fill in the missing values below.

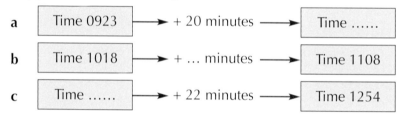

a Time 0923 ──→ + 20 minutes ──→ Time ......

b Time 1018 ──→ + ... minutes ──→ Time 1108

c Time ...... ──→ + 22 minutes ──→ Time 1254

7 Write the following times as a decimal.

a	2h 15m	**b**	3h 45m	**c**	1h 20m
d	3h 30m	**e**	1h 40m	**f**	2h 18m

FM **8** The following timetable shows the times of buses from Hedley to Bottomley.

Hedley	0745	1120	1230	1355	1620	1815
Bottomley	0815	1155	1300	1420	1655	1845

a What time does the bus that gets to Bottomley at 0815 leave Hedley?

b How long does the 1355 bus take to get to Bottomley?

c Moz arrives at the bus stop at Hedley at 1210. How long does she have to wait before the bus arrives?

d The bus fare from Hedley to Bottomley is £1.20 for adults and 60p for children. How much does it cost 3 adults and 2 children to travel on the bus?

9 The clock on the right shows the time 10:25.

Write down two times in the 24-hour clock that could be equivalent to this time.

10 Jonas walks to the station each morning to catch the 0718 train. It takes him 15 minutes to walk to the station. On the way he stops to buy a paper, which takes him 2 minutes. He likes to arrive at the station at least 5 minutes before the train is due. What is the latest time he should leave home?

11 The timetable below shows train times from Leeds to Manchester.

Leeds	0755	0810	0825	0840	0855
Dewsbury	0807	....	0837	....	0907
Huddersfield	0815	0827	0845	0858	0915
Stalybridge	....	0845	....	....	....
Manchester	0852	0905	0923	0937	0950

a How long does the 0755 take to get from Leeds to Manchester?

b How long does the 0810 take to get from Leeds to Manchester?

c Trevor gets to Huddersfield station at 9 am. How long does he have to wait to catch a train to Manchester?

d Mark wants to travel from Dewsbury to Stalybridge.
  i Explain why he will have to change trains at Huddersfield
  ii If he catches the 0807 from Dewsbury, what time will he arrive at Stalybridge?

e Carol lives in Leeds and has to be at a meeting at Manchester University at 10 am. It takes 20 minutes to get from the station to the University. What train should she catch from Leeds to be sure of getting to the meeting on time?

 12 Mobile phone calls are charged at 25p per minute for the first 3 minutes, then 10p per minute for each minute over 3 minutes.

a How much will the following mobile phone calls cost?
  i A call lasting 2 minutes
  ii A call lasting 8 minutes

b After finishing a call, Jonas had a message from the phone company saying 'Your call cost 95p'. How many minutes was the call?

Extension Work

 1 Bradwell school operates a two-week timetable. Year 7 have three 55-minute maths lessons one week and two 1-hour maths lessons in the second week. How much time do they spend in maths over the two weeks?

2 Joan left home at 8:05 am. It took her 8 minutes to walk to Sara's house. Sara took 5 minutes to get ready then they both walked to school, arriving at 8:35. How long did it take them to walk from Sara's house to school?

3 After his birthday, Adam wrote 'thank you' letters to five aunts. He took 1 hour to write the letters. Each letter took the same amount of time to write. How long did it take him to write each letter?

4 Jonas takes 4 minutes to read each page of a comic. The comic has 16 pages. How long will it take him to read it?

5 Sonia was 12 minutes late for a meeting. The meeting lasted 1 hour and 45 minutes and finished at 11:50 am. What time did Sonia arrive at the meeting?

6 The first three periods at Stocksfield school last 1 hour and 45 minutes. Each period is the same length. How long is each period?

LEVEL BOOSTER

3

I can read both 12-hour clocks and 24-hour clocks.

I can change times in the 12-hour clock to times in the 24-hour clock, for example 6:25 pm is 1825h.

I can change times in the 24-hour clock to times in the 12-hour clock, for example 1915h is 7:15 pm.

I know the days in a year, the days in each month and I can read a calendar.

I can work out the difference between two times, for example from 1124 to 1257 is 1 hour and 33 minutes.

I can read a timetable and work out the times of journeys.

I know the decimal equivalents of simple fractions of an hour, for example 15 minutes = 0.25 hours.

4

I can do calculations involving time in real-life situations.

National Test questions

3

1 *2001 3–5 Paper 1*

My clock shows:

The hours and the minutes are both multiples of 3.

multiple of 3   multiple of 3

a Write a **different time** when the hours and the minutes are both multiples of 3.

b Later, my clock shows:

How many minutes will it be before the hours and the minutes are both multiples of 6?

8

2   *2000 3–5 Paper 1*

Look at this time interval:

| Time 10:20 | → + 10 minutes → | Time 10:30 |

Copy and fill in the **missing times**:

a | Time 7:20 | → + 35 minutes → | Time …… |

b | Time 6:27 | → + … minutes → | Time 7:00 |

c | Time …… | → + 40 minutes → | Time 15:00 |

 3   *1998 3–5 Paper 2*

Look at the calendar for the first four months in 1998.

	January				February				
Sunday		4	11	18	25	1	8	15	22
Monday		5	12	19	26	2	9	16	23
Tuesday		6	13	20	27	3	10	17	24
Wednesday		7	14	21	28	4	11	18	25
Thursday	1	8	15	22	29	5	12	19	26
Friday	2	9	16	23	30	6	13	20	27
Saturday	3	10	17	24	31	7	14	21	28

	March				April				
Sunday	1	8	15	22	29	5	12	19	26
Monday	2	9	16	23	30	6	13	20	27
Tuesday	3	10	17	24	31	7	14	21	28
Wednesday	4	11	18	25		1	8	15	22	29
Thursday	5	12	19	26		2	9	16	23	30
Friday	6	13	20	27		3	10	17	24
Saturday	7	14	21	28		4	11	18	25

Monday, February 16th is shaded on the calendar.

a   What was the date of the **third Sunday** in **January**?

b   How many **Sundays** were there altogether in **January**?

c   There were **more Mondays** than **Thursdays** in **March**.

Complete this sentence so that it is correct:

There were more ……….. than …………. in **April**.

d   Jane went swimming on **Wednesday, January 14th**.

She went swimming again **4 weeks later**.

On **what date** did she go swimming the second time?

e   The swimming pool **closed** for repairs on **Friday, March 20th**.

It opened again on **Friday, April 10th**.

For **how many weeks** was the swimming pool shut?

f   Which day in **March** had numbers in the **7 times table** as its dates?

FM **4** *2006 3–5 Paper 2*

There are 12 pupils in a group. The table below gives information about them.

First name	Last name	Male or female?	Date of birth
Alex	Alcroft	M	20.11.92
Helen	Brooks	F	10.01.93
Huw	Davies	M	21.11.92
Ben	Howard	M	24.06.93
Laura	Miller	F	07.12.92
Amy	Pound	F	08.06.93
Surjit	Sandhu	F	03.01.93
Jade	Smith	F	04.09.92
Mike	Smith	M	26.01.93
Leroy	Taylor	M	06.10.92
Claire	White	F	23.09.92
Louise	Wilson	F	26.02.93

Use the table to answer these questions:

a How many **girls** are in the group?

b Whose birthday is **one day after** Alex Alcroft's birthday?

c Who is the **oldest boy** in the group?

d A new pupil, Sue Li, joins the group.

She was born exactly **1 month after** Laura Miller.

What is Sue's date of birth?

FM **5** *2005 3–5 Paper 2*

The diagram shows a heating control.

The arrows show the times the heating control turns on and off.

a Look at the sentences below. Write the missing times.

The heating turns **on** at .... and turns **off** at ....

Altogether the heating is on for .... hours in the morning.

b The heating turns on again in the evening.

It turns **on at 5 pm** and stays on for **6 hours**.

Copy the diagram and **draw two arrows** to show this information.

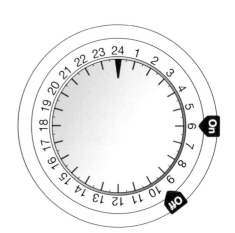

6 *2003 3–5 Paper 1*

a My wall clock shows this time:

Which **two** of the digital clocks below could be showing the **same time** as my wall clock?

b Early in the **morning** my wall clock shows this time:

 morning

My digital clock shows the same time as my wall clock.

Write what time my digital clock is showing.

c In the **afternoon** my wall clock shows this time:

 afternoon

My digital clock is a 24-hour clock.

Now what time is my digital clock showing?

 7 *2002 3-5 Paper 1*

How much does it cost to park for **40 minutes**?

Show your working.

This chapter is going to show you

- Some simple number patterns that you may have seen before, and how to describe them
- How to make up sequences and describe them using basic algebra

What you should already know

- Odd and even numbers
- Times tables up to 10×10

Sequences and rules

You can make up many different sequences with whole numbers using simple rules.

Example 2.1 ▷

Rule [add 3] Starting at 1 gives the sequence
$$1, \quad 4, \quad 7, \quad 10, \quad 13, \ldots$$
with $+3$ between each term.

Starting at 2 gives the sequence
$$2, \quad 5, \quad 8, \quad 11, \quad 14, \ldots$$
with $+3$ between each term.

Rule [double] Starting at 1 gives the sequence
$$1, \quad 2, \quad 4, \quad 8, \quad 16, \ldots$$
with $\times 2$ between each term.

Starting at 3 gives the sequence
$$3, \quad 6, \quad 12, \quad 24, \quad 48, \ldots$$
with $\times 2$ between each term.

So you see, with *different* **rules** and *different* **starting points**, you can make millions of *different* **sequences**.

The numbers in a sequence are called **terms**. The starting point is called the **1st term**. The rule is called the **term-to-term rule**.

Exercise 2A

① Use each term-to-term rule and starting point to make a sequence with four terms in it.

a Rule [add 3] Start at 2. **b** Rule [multiply by 3] Start at 1.

c Rule [add 5] Start at 4. **d** Rule [multiply by 10] Start at 2.

e Rule [add 9] Start at 6. **f** Rule [multiply by 5] Start at 2.

g Rule [add 7] Start at 3. **h** Rule [multiply by 2] Start at 5.

② Describe the term-to-term rule of each sequence below. Use this rule to write down the next two terms in each sequence.

a 2, 4, 6, … **b** 3, 6, 9, … **c** 1, 10, 100, … **d** 2, 10, 50, …
e 0, 7, 14, … **f** 4, 9, 14, … **g** 9, 18, 27, … **h** 12, 24, 36, …

③ Each of these sequences uses an 'add' rule. Copy and complete the sequences.

a 2, 5, 8, ☐, ☐, 17 **b** 1, 6, ☐, 16, ☐, ☐

c 5, ☐, ☐, 11, ☐, ☐ **d** ☐, 14, ☐, ☐, 29, ☐

④ Each of these sequences uses a 'multiply by' rule. Copy and complete the sequences.

a 1, 10, ☐, ☐, 10 000 **b** 3, ☐, ☐, 24, 48, ☐

c ☐, ☐, ☐, 16, 32, ☐ **d** 4, ☐, ☐, 108, 324

Extension **Work**

1 For each pair of numbers given below, find at least two different sequences. Then write the next two terms. In each case, describe the term-to-term rule you have used.

a 1, 4, … **b** 3, 9, … **c** 2, 6, …
d 3, 6, … **e** 4, 8, … **f** 5, 15, …

2 Find at least one sequence between each pair of numbers given below. In each case, describe the term-to-term rule you have used.

a 1, …, 8 **b** 1, …, 12 **c** 5, …, 15
d 4, …, 10 **e** 10, …, 20 **f** 16, …, 20

Finding terms in patterns

In any sequence, you will have a 1st term, 2nd term, 3rd term, 4th term and so on.

Example 2.2 ▷ Look at the pattern of matches below.

     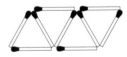

Pattern 1   Pattern 2   Pattern 3   Pattern 4
3 matches   5 matches   7 matches   9 matches

I could easily draw the next pattern and count that it has 11 matches and carry on doing this for as many patterns as I like.

Pattern 5
11 matches

Example 2.2
continued

A better way is to put the numbers into a table, spot the term-to-term rule and use this to work out the number of matches.

Pattern	Matches
1	3
2	5
3	7
4	9
5	11

This table can be carried on as far as I like, but there is an easier way to work out the number of matches in, for example, the 10th pattern.

The term-to-term rule is 'add 2'. To get from the 5th pattern to the 10th pattern, I need to add on 2 five more times, i.e. $11 + 2 \times 5 = 11 + 10 = 21$.

So there are 21 matches in the 10th pattern.

Exercise 2B

For each of the series of diagrams below, draw the next diagram, fill in a table showing the number of matches in the first 5 patterns and work out how many matches there are in the 10th and 20th patterns.

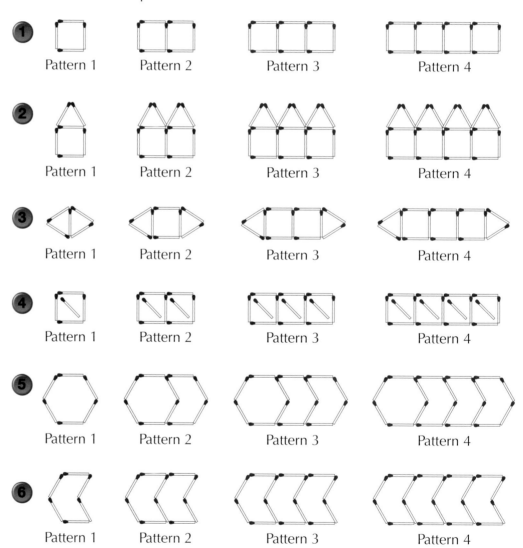

1

Pattern 1   Pattern 2   Pattern 3   Pattern 4

2

Pattern 1   Pattern 2   Pattern 3   Pattern 4

3

Pattern 1   Pattern 2   Pattern 3   Pattern 4

4

Pattern 1   Pattern 2   Pattern 3   Pattern 4

5

Pattern 1   Pattern 2   Pattern 3   Pattern 4

6

Pattern 1   Pattern 2   Pattern 3   Pattern 4

Extension Work

1 How many dots will be in: **a** the 5th pattern? **b** the 10th pattern?

Pattern 1   Pattern 2   Pattern 3   Pattern 4

2 How many dots will be in: **a** the 5th pattern? **b** the 10th pattern?

Pattern 1   Pattern 2   Pattern 3   Pattern 4

3 How many squares will be in: **a** the 5th pattern? **b** the 10th pattern?

Pattern 1   Pattern 2   Pattern 3   Pattern 4

Function machines

Example 2.3 Fill in the output box of this function machine.

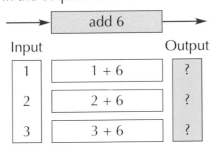

Input	add 6	Output
1	1 + 6	?
2	2 + 6	?
3	3 + 6	?

The output box is

7
8
9

Exercise 2C

1 Find the missing inputs or outputs for each function machine shown below.

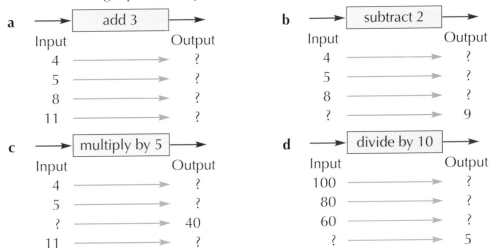

a add 3

Input	Output
4	?
5	?
8	?
11	?

b subtract 2

Input	Output
4	?
5	?
8	?
?	9

c multiply by 5

Input	Output
4	?
5	?
?	40
11	?

d divide by 10

Input	Output
100	?
80	?
60	?
?	5

2 Give each function below in words.

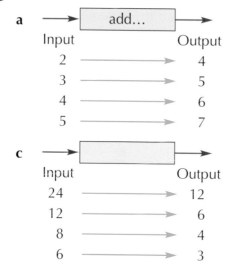

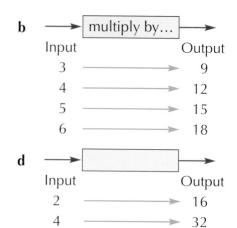

a add...

Input	Output
2	4
3	5
4	6
5	7

b multiply by...

Input	Output
3	9
4	12
5	15
6	18

c

Input	Output
24	12
12	6
8	4
6	3

d

Input	Output
2	16
4	32
6	48
8	64

3 Find the missing inputs or outputs for each function machine shown below.

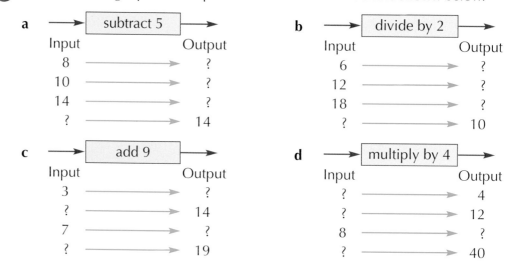

a subtract 5

Input	Output
8	?
10	?
14	?
?	14

b divide by 2

Input	Output
6	?
12	?
18	?
?	10

c add 9

Input	Output
3	?
?	14
7	?
?	19

d multiply by 4

Input	Output
?	4
?	12
8	?
?	40

4 Make up your own diagrams to show each of these functions.

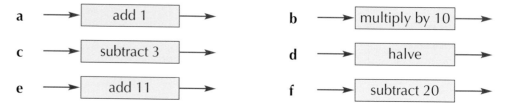

a add 1

b multiply by 10

c subtract 3

d halve

e add 11

f subtract 20

Find at least ten different functions that have 50 as one of the output numbers.

Double function machines

Example 2.4 ▷ Fill in the output box of this double function machine.

Input	multiply by 2		add 5	Output
3	... × 2 = 6	6	... + 5 =	?
5	... × 2 = 10	10	... + 5 =	?
7	... × 2 = 14	14	... + 5 =	?

The output box is

11
15
19

Exercise 2D

(1) Find the outputs for each of these double function machines.

a

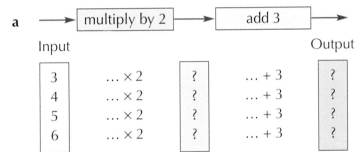

Input	multiply by 2		add 3	Output
3	... × 2	?	... + 3	?
4	... × 2	?	... + 3	?
5	... × 2	?	... + 3	?
6	... × 2	?	... + 3	?

b

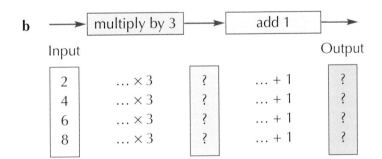

Input	multiply by 3		add 1	Output
2	... × 3	?	... + 1	?
4	... × 3	?	... + 1	?
6	... × 3	?	... + 1	?
8	... × 3	?	... + 1	?

c

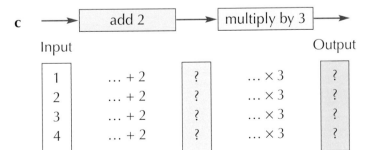

Input	add 2		multiply by 3	Output
1	... + 2	?	... × 3	?
2	... + 2	?	... × 3	?
3	... + 2	?	... × 3	?
4	... + 2	?	... × 3	?

3

d

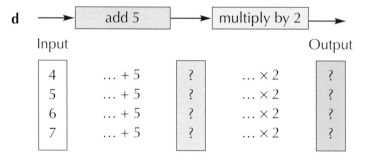

Input				Output
4	... + 5	?	... × 2	?
5	... + 5	?	... × 2	?
6	... + 5	?	... × 2	?
7	... + 5	?	... × 2	?

2 Draw diagrams to illustrate each of these double function machines. Choose your own four input numbers.

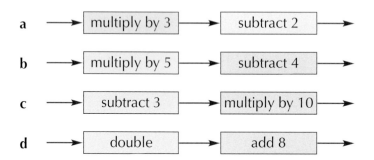

3 Look at the double functions below. Copy and fill in the boxes with missing functions or numbers.

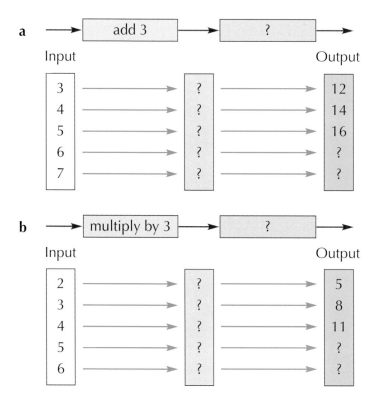

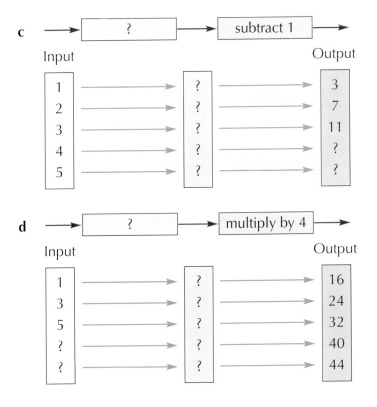

c

Input		Output
1	?	3
2	?	7
3	?	11
4	?	?
5	?	?

d   ? → multiply by 4 →

Input		Output
1	?	16
3	?	24
5	?	32
?	?	40
?	?	44

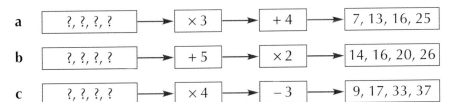

4 Work backwards from each output to find the input to each of these functions.

a ?, ?, ?, ? → × 3 → + 4 → 7, 13, 16, 25

b ?, ?, ?, ? → + 5 → × 2 → 14, 16, 20, 26

c ?, ?, ?, ? → × 4 → − 3 → 9, 17, 33, 37

Each of these functions is made up from two operations, as in Question 3.
Find each double function.

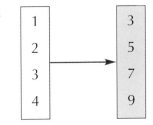

a

1	3
2	5
3	7
4	9

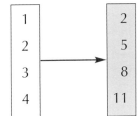

b

1	2
2	5
3	8
4	11

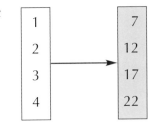

c

1	7
2	12
3	17
4	22

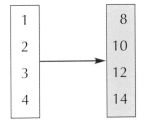

d

1	8
2	10
3	12
4	14

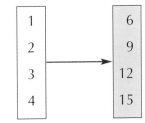

e

1	6
2	9
3	12
4	15

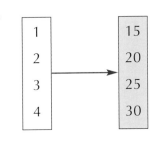

f

1	15
2	20
3	25
4	30

Using letter symbols to represent functions

The rule in the operation box of a function machine can be written using the letter n, which stands for 'any number'.

Example 2.5

Fill in the output box of this function machine.

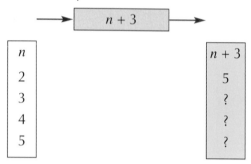

The output box is

| 5 |
| 6 |
| 7 |
| 8 |

Exercise 2E

(1) Copy each function below. Then find the outputs.

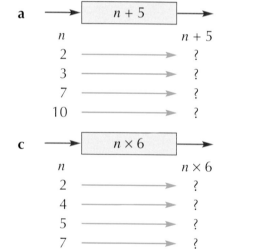

a

n	$n + 5$
2	?
3	?
7	?
10	?

b

n	$n \times 3$
4	?
5	?
8	?
11	?

c

n	$n \times 6$
2	?
4	?
5	?
7	?

d

n	$n - 3$
5	?
9	?
14	?
20	?

(2) Write each function using n, as in Question 1.

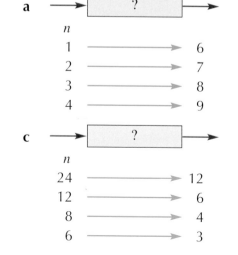

a

n	?
1	6
2	7
3	8
4	9

b

n	?
5	3
6	4
7	5
8	6

c

n	?
24	12
12	6
8	4
6	3

d

n	?
2	16
4	32
6	48
8	64

(3) Write each function using n, as in Question 2.

a

2 → 9
3 → 10
4 → 11
5 → 12

b

2 → 10
3 → 15
4 → 20
5 → 25

c

2 → 1
3 → 2
4 → 3
5 → 4

d

2 → 8
3 → 12
4 → 16
5 → 20

e

12 → 4
15 → 5
21 → 7
30 → 10

f

2 → 7
3 → 8
4 → 9
5 → 10

g

2 → 20
3 → 30
4 → 40
5 → 50

h

12 → 9
13 → 10
14 → 11
15 → 12

(4) Draw some diagrams with your own numbers to show these functions.

a ⟶ $n + 7$ ⟶   **b** ⟶ $5 \times n$ ⟶

c ⟶ $n - 3$ ⟶   **d** ⟶ $10 \times n$ ⟶

e ⟶ $n + 9$ ⟶   **f** ⟶ $n - 4$ ⟶

g ⟶ $n + 11$ ⟶   **h** ⟶ $7 \times n$ ⟶

Extension Work

Find at least ten different functions using the letter n, and a value for n, that have an output number of 100. For example:

$n + 5$ with an input of 95

A function investigation

This is an investigation of a double function using a two-digit whole number.

Examples of two-digit whole numbers are 12, 36, 45, 71, 98.

The function is:

⟶ multiply the two digits ⟶ add the result to the sum of the two digits ⟶

For example:

23 ⟶ $2 \times 3 = 6$ ⟶ $6 + 2 + 3$ ⟶ 11

You can now investigate!

1 ● Start with any two-digit whole number. Use the above function to get a new number.

   ● When the new number is not a two-digit number, stop.

   ● When the new number is a two-digit number, repeat the function to get another new number.

   ● Keep repeating this until you cannot get a two-digit number. You then stop. For example:

   83 → (24 + 8 + 3) = **35** → (15 + 3 + 5) = **23** → (6 + 2 + 3) = **11** → (1 + 1 + 1) = **3**

2 Try at least ten different two-digit whole numbers. See how long their chains are before they stop.

3 Some chains carry on for ever. Which ones are they?

4 Which is the number you stop on most?

5 How long is the longest chain, apart from those that never end?

6 Try changing the function to see what happens.

LEVEL BOOSTER

3 I can find the output value for function machines like the ones below when I know the input value.

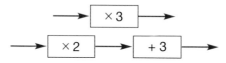

4 I can write down a sequence given the first term, say 3, and a term-to-term rule such as 'goes up by 4 each time', i.e. 3, 7, 11, 15, 19, ….

I can give the term-to-term rule for a sequence such as 4, 7, 10, 13, 16, …, i.e. 'goes up by 3 each time'.

I can write an algebraic expressions for a rule such as 'add 3', i.e. $x + 3$.

I can find the operation in a function machine like the one below when I am given the inputs and outputs, i.e. × 4.

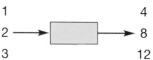

5 I can find any term in a sequence given the first term, say 5, and the term-to-term rule such as 'goes up by 6 each time', i.e. the 20th term is 119.

1 *2003 3–5 Paper 1*

a The number chain below is part of a **doubling** number chain.

What are the two missing numbers?

b The number chain below is part of a **halving** number chain.

What are the two missing numbers?

2 *2005 3–5 Paper 2*

Here is a sequence of shapes made with grey and white tiles.

Shape Number 1	Shape Number 2	Shape Number 3	Shape Number 4

The number of grey tiles = 2 × the shape number
The number of white tiles = 2 × the shape number

a Altogether, how many tiles will there be in shape number **5**?

b Altogether, how many tiles will there be in shape number **15**?

c Write down the missing number from this sentence:

The **total** number of tiles = ☐ × the shape number.

3 *2006 3–5 Paper 2*

a These rules show how to get from one number to the next in these sequences.

Use the rules to write the next **two** numbers in each sequence.

Rule:	**Add 8**	4	12	☐	☐
Rule:	**Multiply by 3**	4	12	☐	☐
Rule:	**Divide by 4 then add 11**	4	12	☐	☐

b A sequence of numbers starts like this: 30   22   18

Could the rule be **Subtract 8**?

Explain your answer.

Valencia Planetarium

Use this key to answer the following questions.

Ladders and grids are made from combinations of:

'L' links   'T' links   'X' links   'R' rods

Each combination can be expressed algebraically.

For example:

4L + 2T + 7R   4L + 6T + 2X + 17R

1 Look at the ladders on the right.

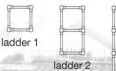

ladder 1

ladder 2

ladder 3

a Write down algebraic expressions for each of them.

b Copy and fill in this table.

Ladder	L links	T links	R Rods
1	4	0	4
2	4	2	7
3			

c Continue the table to find the number of links and rods up to ladder 7.

d Write down an algebraic expression for the links and rods in ladder 8.

2 Look at the following rectangles that are 2 squares deep.

i   **ii**   **iii**

a Write down algebraic expressions for each of them.

b Copy and complete the following table.

Rectangle	L links	T links	X links	R Rods
2 × 1	4	2	0	7
2 × 2	4	4	1	12
2 × 3				

c Continue the table to find the number of links and rods in a 2 × 7 rectangle.

d Write down an algebraic expression for the links and rods in a 2 × 8 rectangle.

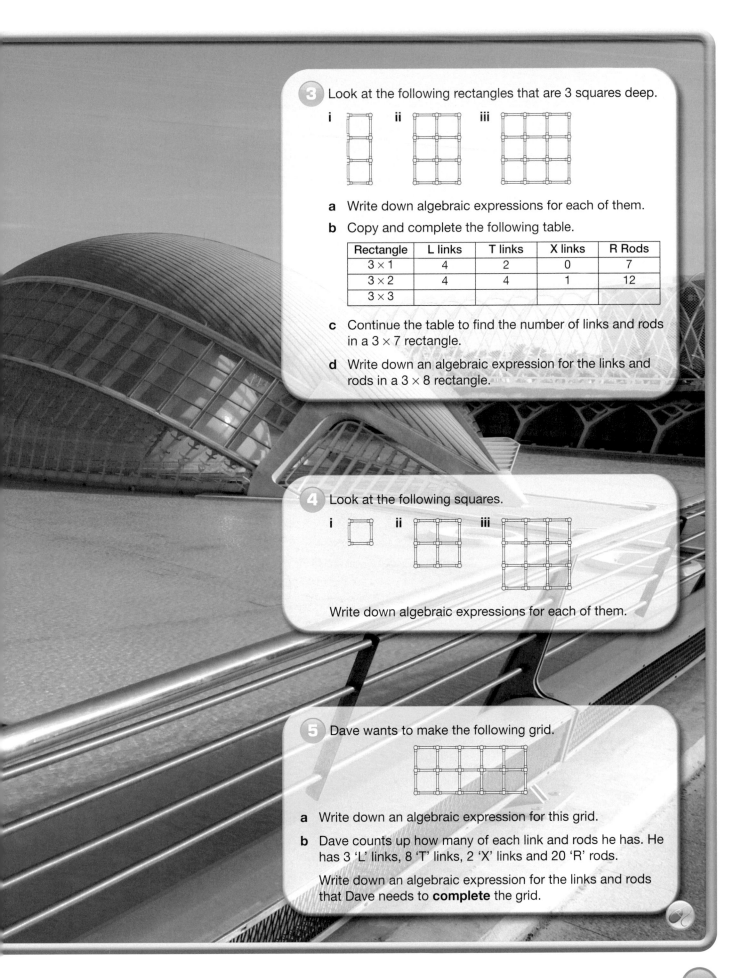

3 Look at the following rectangles that are 3 squares deep.

i   ii   iii

a Write down algebraic expressions for each of them.

b Copy and complete the following table.

Rectangle	L links	T links	X links	R Rods
3 × 1	4	2	0	7
3 × 2	4	4	1	12
3 × 3				

c Continue the table to find the number of links and rods in a 3 × 7 rectangle.

d Write down an algebraic expression for the links and rods in a 3 × 8 rectangle.

4 Look at the following squares.

i   ii   iii

Write down algebraic expressions for each of them.

5 Dave wants to make the following grid.

a Write down an algebraic expression for this grid.

b Dave counts up how many of each link and rods he has. He has 3 'L' links, 8 'T' links, 2 'X' links and 20 'R' rods.

Write down an algebraic expression for the links and rods that Dave needs to **complete** the grid.

CHAPTER **3** Number **2**

This chapter is going to show you	What you should already know
● How to do real life problems with money ● Some simple number patterns that you may have seen before, and how to describe them ● How to create sequences and describe them in words ● How to generate and describe simple whole-number sequences	● The coins in use in Britain today ● Odd and even numbers ● Times tables up to 10×10

Currency

Britain uses a system of decimal currency. The main unit of currency is the pound, which is divided into 100 pence.

The main coins in use are:

1p   2p   5p   10p   20p   50p   £1   £2

There are also £5, £10, £20 and £50 notes.

Different combinations of coins can be used to make different amounts of money. For example, there are two ways to make 3p:

1p + 1p + 1p or **2p + 1p**.

There are four ways to make 5p:

1p + 1p + 1p + 1p + 1p or **1p + 1p + 1p + 2p** or **1p + 2p + 2p** or **5p**.

Example 3.1 ▷ Show that there are 6 different ways to make 7p using coins.

The coins that could be used are 1p, 2p and 5p, so the combinations are:

1p + 1p + 1p + 1p + 1p + 1p + 1p or **1p + 1p + 1p + 1p + 1p + 2p**

or **1p + 1p + 1p + 2p + 2p** or **1p + 2p + 2p + 2p** or **1p + 1p + 5p** or **2p + 5p**

Example 3.2 ▷ Show that there is only one way to make 12p using exactly 4 coins.

The only combination is **1p + 1p + 5p + 5p**

Example 3.3 ▷ You have lots of 10p and 2p coins.

a   Explain why it is not possible to make an odd number of pence with these coins.

b   There are 6 ways to make 50p using just 10p and 2p coins.

One way is **5 × 10p** and **0 × 2p**

Complete a table to show all the other ways.

10p coins   2p coins

a   You cannot make an odd number of pence, as both 10p and 2p are even, so any combination will also be even.

b
10p coins	2p coins
5	0
4	5
3	10
2	15
1	20
0	25

Exercise 3A

1 Using just 1p and 2p coins, write down all the ways of making a total of 4 pence.

2 Using just 2p and 5p coins write down all the ways of making a total of 12 pence.

3 Mark buys a magazine for 25p and receives 75p change from a £1 coin. He receives exactly 4 coins. What coins are they?

4 Zara has two 20p coins, one 2p coin and a 1p coin.

Ali has a 50p coin, a 10p coin and a 5p coin.

Ali owes Zara 24p. Explain how he can pay her.

Zara

Ali

5 What is the smallest number of coins that you need to make a total of 68 pence?

6 Don and Donna have the same amount of money as each other. Don has two coins which are the same, and Donna has five coins which are the same. What could their coins be?

7 A purse contains the same number of 1p, 5p and 10p coins. In total, the purse contains £1.44. How many of each type of coin are there?

8 A purse contains 3 times as many 20p coins as 1p coins. In total, the purse contains £1.83. How many of each coin are there?

9 Art has three coins which are the same. Bart has five coins which are the same. Explain why it is not possible for them to have the same amount of money.

FM **10** Grapes cost 54p a kilogram. I buy 1½ kilograms and pay with a £1. I receive 4 coins in my change. What coins do I get?

FM **11** I buy two cans of cola for 37p per can and pay with a £1. I receive 3 coins in my change. What coins do I get?

FM **12** I buy 3 pencils for 21p each and pay with a £1. I receive 4 coins in my change. What coins do I get?

Extension **Work**

In the USA, the coins are 1 cent, 5 cents, 10 cents and 25 cents. These are known as pennies, nickels, dimes and quarters.

1 Mario has $1.17 in pennies, nickels and dimes. He has a total of 25 coins. There are twice as many nickels as pennies, so how many of each kind of coin does Mario have?

2 Joss has 35 coins which consist of nickels, dimes and quarters. The coins are worth $5.55. She has 5 more dimes than nickels. How many nickels, dimes and quarters does she have?

Decimals

Look at this picture. What do the decimal numbers mean? How would you say them?

When you multiply by 10, all the digits are moved one place to the left.

Example 3.4 ▷ Work out 3.5×10.

Hundreds	Tens	Units	Tenths	Hundredths
		3	● 5	
	3	5	●	

When you divide by 10, all the digits move one place to the right.

Example 3.5 ▷ Work out $23 \div 10$.

Hundreds	Tens	Units	Tenths	Hundredths
	2	3 ●		
		2	● 3	

Exercise 3B

1 Eight of these numbers are divisible by 10. Write them down.

| 40 | 55 | 20 | 26 | 50 | 35 | 29 | 110 |
| 46 | 10 | 500 | 625 | 370 | 690 | 41 | |

2 Eight of these numbers are divisible by 100. Write them down.

| 712 | 320 | 40 | 550 | 800 | 25 | 1200 | 600 |
| 6200 | 300 | 4000 | 617 | 1000 | 670 | 250 000 | |

3 Without using a calculator, work out the following.

a 4×10

b 89×10

c 7×100

d 41×100

e $30 \div 10$

f $8900 \div 10$

g $700 \div 10$

h $400 \div 100$

i $5800 \div 100$

4 Find the missing number in each case.

a $3 \times 10 = \boxed{}$ **b** $3 \times \boxed{} = 30$

c $3 \div 10 = \boxed{}$ **d** $3 \div \boxed{} = 0.3$

5 Without using a calculator, work out the following.

a 4.5×10 **b** 0.6×10 **c** 5.3×10 **d** 0.03×10

e 5.8×10 **f** 0.7×10 **g** $4.5 \div 10$ **h** $0.6 \div 10$

i $5.3 \div 10$ **j** $0.03 \div 10$ **k** $5.8 \div 10$ **l** $0.04 \div 10$

m $5.01 \div 10$ **n** 6.378×10

6 Find the missing number in each case.

a $0.3 \times 10 = \boxed{}$ **b** $0.3 \times \boxed{} = 30$

c $0.3 \div 10 = \boxed{}$ **d** $0.3 \div \boxed{} = 0.03$

e $\boxed{} \div 10 = 0.03$ **f** $\boxed{} \div 10 = 30$

g $\boxed{} \times 10 = 30\,000$ **h** $\boxed{} \times 10 = 300$

 7 Copy, complete and work out the total of this shopping bill:

10 chews at £0.03 each   =

10 packets of mints at £0.23 each   =

10 cans of pop at £0.99 each   =

Extension Work

Design a poster to explain clearly how to multiply a number by 10 and how to divide a number by 10.

Ordering whole numbers and decimals

Name	Leroy	Myrtle	Jack	Baby Jane	Alf	Doris
Age	37	21	32	1 year	57	68
Height	170 cm	154 cm	189 cm	34 cm	102 cm	180 cm
Weight	75 kg	50 kg	68 kg	8 kg	60 kg	76 kg

Look at the people in the picture. How would you put them in order?

When you compare the size of numbers, you have to consider the **place value** of each digit.

It helps if you fill in the numbers in a table like the one shown on the right.

Thousands	Hundreds	Tens	Units
	2	3	3
	2	0	3
2	3	0	4

Example 3.6

Put the numbers 233, 203 and 2304 in order, from smallest to largest.

The numbers are shown in the table.

Working across the table from the left, you can see that the last number has a digit in the thousands column. The other two numbers have the same digit in the hundreds column, but the first number has the larger digit in the tens column. So, the order is:

203, 233 and 2304

Example 3.7

Put 3, 14, 5, 8 in order of size, using the sign <.

The answer is:

$3 < 5 < 8 < 14$

with the smallest number put first.

Example 3.8

Which is bigger, 329 or 392?

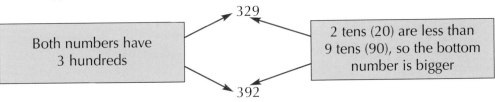

So, you write: 329 < 392.

1 a Copy the table above (but not the numbers). Write the following numbers in the table, placing each digit in the correct column.

457   45   4057   4   450   5   405

b Use your answer to part **a** to write the numbers in order from smallest to largest.

2 Put these numbers in *ascending* order (from smallest to largest).

a   29   69   47   75   70   **b**   907   98   203   302   92

3 Put these numbers in *descending* order (from largest to smallest).

a   45   403   54   450   400   **b**   513   315   135   2531   153

4 Edinburgh is 202 miles from Leeds. York is 24 miles from Leeds.

Which of these two cities is the greater distance from Leeds?

5 Aberdeen is 513 miles from Bristol. Fort William is 491 miles from Bristol.
Which of these two towns is the lesser distance from Bristol?

6 Manchester is 39 miles from Sheffield. Nottingham is 44 miles from Sheffield.
   a Which of these two cities is the further from Sheffield?
   b How much further is it?

7 John Smith earns £32 429.
Fred Davies earns £32 294.
Joe Bloggs earns £33 003.
   a Who earns the most?   **b** Who earns the least?

8 Put the correct sign, > or <, between each pair of numbers.
   a 315 ... 325   **b** 420 ... 402   **c** 6780 ... 6709
   d 525 ... 5225   **e** 345 ... 400   **f** 472 ... 427

9 Put these amounts of money in order.
   a 56p   £1.25   £0.60   130p   £0.07
   b £0.04   £1.04   101p   35p   £0.37

Extension **Work**

When you compare times, lengths and weights, you must use the *same* units
in each comparison.

1 Put these times in order: 1 hour 10 minutes, 25 minutes, 1.25 hours, 0.5 hours.

2 One metre is 100 centimetres. Change all the lengths below to metres
and then put them in order from smallest to largest.
   6.25 m   269 cm   32 cm   2.7 m   0.34 m

3 One kilogram is 1000 grams. Change all the weights below to kilograms
and then put them in order from smallest to largest.
   467 g   1.260 kg   56 g   0.5 kg   0.055 kg

4 Write each of the following statements in words.
   a 3.1 < 3.14 < 3.142   **b** £0.07 < 32p < £0.56

Directed numbers

Temperature 32 °C
Latitude 17° South
Time 09 30 h GMT

Temperature −13 °C
Latitude 84° North
Time 23 30 h GMT

Look at the two pictures. What are the differences between the temperatures, the latitudes
and the times?

All numbers have a sign. Positive numbers have a + sign in front of them although we do not always write it. Negative (or minus) numbers have a – sign in front of them. We *always* write the negative sign.

The positions of positive and negative numbers can be put on a number line, as below.

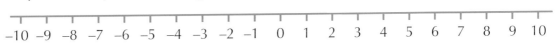

This is very useful, as it helps us to compare positive and negative numbers and also to add and subtract them.

Example 3.9

Which is bigger, –7 or –3?

Because –3 is further to the right on the line, it is the larger number. We can write –7 < –3.

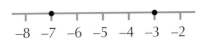

Example 3.10

Work out the answers to   **a**   3 – 2 – 5   **b**   –3 – 5 + 4 – 2

a   Starting at zero and 'jumping' along the number line gives an answer of –4.

b   –3 – 5 + 4 – 2 = –6

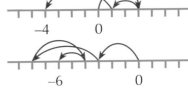

Example 3.11

–3 < 6 means 'negative 3 is less than 6'.

–4 > –7 means 'negative 4 is greater than negative 7'.

State whether these are true or false:

a   7 > 9   **b**   –2 > –1   **c**   –2 > – 5

Marking each of the pairs on a number line, we can see that **a** is false, **b** is false and **c** is true.

Exercise 3D

1 a   Circle each whole number greater than 0 and less than 7.

> –5   –4   –3   –2   –1   0   1   2   3   4   5   6   7   8   9   10

b   Circle each whole number greater than –4 and less than 2.

> –5   –4   –3   –2   –1   0   1   2   3   4   5   6   7   8   9   10

2   State whether each of these is true (T) or false (F).

a   9 > 7   **b**   9 < 16   **c**   5 < –6   **d**   –6 > –4   **e**   –3 < –2

3   Put <, > or = into each ☐ to make a true sentence.

a   5 ☐ 9   **b**   4 ☐ 15   **c**   59 ☐ 48   **d**   13 ☐ 12

e   Two hundred and two ☐ 202   **f**   Two thousand and two ☐ 202

4 Put the correct sign, > or <, between each pair of numbers.

    a −5 … 4   **b** −7 … −10   **c** 3 … −3   **d** −12 … −2

5 Find the number that is halfway between each pair of numbers.

    a −8   −2   **b** −6   +3   **c** −9   −1

6 Work out the answer to each of these.

    a 6 − 9   **b** 2 − 7   **c** 1 − 3   **d** 4 − 4

    e −6 + 9   **f** −7 − 3   **g** −2 − 3   **h** −14 + 7

    i −2 − 3 + 4   **j** −1 + 1 − 2   **k** −3 + 4 − 7   **l** −102 + 103 − 5

7 Find the missing number to make each of these true.

    a +2 − 6 = ☐   **b** +4 + ☐ = +7   **c** −4 + ☐ = 0

    d +5 − ☐ = −1   **e** ☐ + 3 + 4 = ☐   **f** ☐ − 5 = +7

    g ☐ − 5 = +2   **h** +6 − ☐ = 0   **i** ☐ + 5 = −2

    j +2 − 2 = ☐   **k** ☐ − 2 = − 4   **l** ☐ − 2 − 4 = ☐

 8 **a** A fish is 10 m below the surface of the water. A fish eagle is 15 m above the water. How many metres must he descend to get the fish?

    b Alf has £25 in the bank. He writes a cheque for £35. How much has he got in the bank now?

9 In a magic square, the numbers in any row, column or diagonal add up to give the same answer. Copy and complete each of these magic squares.

    a

−7	0	−8
−2		−3

    b

−2		−4
		−3
		−8

Extension **Work**

A maths test consists of 20 questions. Three points are given for a correct answer and two points are deducted when an answer is wrong or not attempted.

Work out the scores for the following people:

    a Aisha gets 12 right and 8 wrong.   **b** Bill gets 10 right and 10 wrong.

    c Charles gets 8 right and 12 wrong.   **d** Dilash gets 9 right and 11 wrong.

What times table are all your answers in?

What happens if there are four points for a right answer and minus two for a wrong answer?

A computer spreadsheet is useful for this activity.

Estimates

UNITED v CITY

CROWD	41 923
SCORE	2 – 1
TIME OF FIRST GOAL	42 min 13 sec
PRICE OF A PIE	95p
CHILDREN	33% off normal ticket prices

Which of the numbers above can be approximated? Which need to be given exactly?

Example 3.12 ▷ Round off the following numbers to the nearest: **i** 10   **ii** 100

    a 431   **b** 578   **c** 705

i Look at the last digit. If it is under 5 round down the number. If it is 5 or over round up the number.

    a 431 ≈ 430   **b** 578 ≈ 580   **c** 705 ≈ 710

ii Look at the tens digit and round up or down as before.

    a 431 ≈ 400   **b** 578 ≈ 600   **c** 705 ≈ 700

Example 3.13 ▷ Round off the following numbers to the nearest whole number.

    a 3.455   **b** 2.76   **c** 7.5

Look at the number after the decimal point (the tenths digit). Round down if it is under 5 and up if it is 5 or over.

    a 3.455 ≈ 3   **b** 2.76 ≈ 3   **c** 7.5 ≈ 8

Exercise 3E

1 The line shows the ages of members of a family.

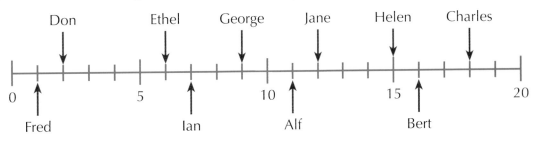

Copy and complete this table.

Name	Alf	Bert	Charles	Don	Ethel	Fred	George	Helen	Ian	Jane
Age										
Age to nearest 10 years										

3

2 The price of a dishwasher is £435.

    a What is the washer's price to the nearest £100?

    b What is the washer's price to the nearest £10?

3 The price of a bike is £282.

    a What is its price to the nearest £100?

    b What is its price to the nearest £10?

4 The price of a hi-fi is £467.

    a What is its price to the nearest £100?

    b What is the price to the nearest £50?

    c What is the price to the nearest £10?

5 These are the attendances at FA cup matches. Copy and complete the table.

Game		Attendance	Attendance to nearest 100	Attendance to nearest 1000
a	Charlton v Walsall	18 573	18 600	
b	Chelsea v West Ham	33 443		
c	Everton v Leyton Orient	35 851		36 000
d	Gillingham v Bristol Rovers	17 624		
e	Preston v Sheffield United	13 068		
f	Rotherham v Crewe	8 477	8500	
g	Tottenham v Bolton	26 820		
h	York v Fulham	7 563		

6 Round each of these numbers to the nearest whole number.

    a 3.27   **b** 6.72   **c** 2.351

    d 9.85   **e** 4.032   **f** 7.43

7 Which is the best approximation for 50.7 − 39.2?

    a 506 − 392   **b** 51 − 39   **c** 50 − 39   **d** 5.06 − 3.92

8 Which is the best approximation for 19.3×42.6?

    a 20×40 **b** 19×42 **c** 19×40 **d** 20×42

9 Which is the best estimate for $54.6 \div 10.9$?

    a $500 \div 100$ **b** $54 \div 11$ **c** $50 \div 11$ **d** $55 \div 11$

10 Estimate the number the arrow is pointing to.

    a    **b**    **c**

Extension Work

Using a calculator, write down lots of multiplication sums such as $23 \times 42 = 966$.

When you have about 10 calculations, look at the last digit of each number.
For example:

    $23 \times 42 = 966$

See if you can spot a rule about the connection between the last digits.

By looking at the following calculations, say which of them *must be* wrong.

    a $54 \times 44 = 2376$ **b** $36 \times 23 = 882$ **c** $17 \times 34 = 587$

    d $16 \times 42 = 672$ **e** $58 \times 18 = 1046$ **f** $65 \times 25 = 1625$

Column method for addition and subtraction

Look at the picture. What is wrong?

You may have several ways of adding and subtracting numbers, such as estimation or using a number line. Here you will be shown how to set out additions and subtractions using the column method.

Example 3.14 ▷ Work out, without using a calculator: **a** 327 + 148 **b** 428 − 345

a Write the numbers in columns.

$$
\begin{array}{r}
327 \\
+\ 148 \\
\hline
475 \\
{}_{1}
\end{array}
$$

Note the carry digit in the units column, because 7 + 8 = 15.

b Write the numbers in columns.

$$
\begin{array}{r}
^{3}\!\!\not4^{1}28 \\
-\ 345 \\
\hline
83
\end{array}
$$

Note that, because you cannot take 4 from 2 in the tens column, you have to borrow from the hundreds column. This means that 4 becomes 3 and 2 becomes 12.

Example 3.15 ▷ Work out 514 + 145 − 372.

This type of problem needs to be done in two stages. First, do the addition and then do the subtraction.

$$
\begin{array}{r}
514 \\
+\ 145 \\
\hline
659
\end{array}
\qquad
\begin{array}{r}
^{5}\!\not6^{1}59 \\
-\ 372 \\
\hline
287
\end{array}
$$

3

Exercise 3F

1 By means of a drawing, show how you could use a number line to work out the answers to these.

a 24 + 35	**b** 56 + 64	**c** 53 + 745	**d** 463 + 98
e 84 − 53	**f** 91 − 18	**g** 137 − 49	**h** 940 − 486

2 Repeat the calculations in Question 1 using the column method. Show all your working.

3 Use the column method to work out each of the following additions.

a 371 + 142	**b** 326 + 1573	**c** 678 + 459	**d** 962 + 70
e 479 + 120	**f** 608 + 216	**g** 12 + 341 + 456	
h 7657 + 3125 + 608			

4 Use the column method to work out each of the following subtractions.

a 371 − 142	**b** 326 − 157	**c** 678 − 459	**d** 962 − 70
e 479 − 12	**f** 608 − 216	**g** 120 + 341 − 456	
h 7657 + 3125 − 608			

FM **5** Work out the cost of a pair of socks at £5, a pair of laces at 80p, a tin of shoe polish at £1 and two shoe brushes at £1.50 each.

6 Write down the change you would get from £10 if you bought goods worth:

    a £4.50   **b** £3.99   **c** £7.01   **d** 40p

Extension Work

If you are given any one of these facts, you should be able to write down the other three facts. For example:

$$40 + 36 = 76 \text{ tells you that } 36 + 40 = 76$$
$$76 - 36 = 40$$
$$76 - 40 = 36$$

1 $147 + 206 = 353$. Write down the three number facts related to this.

2 $481 - 217 = 264$. Write down the three number facts related to this.

3 $584 + 162 = 746$. Fill in the answers below.

    $746 - 584 =$ $746 - 162 =$

4 $507 - 168 = 339$. Fill in the answers below.

    $339 + 168 =$ $507 - 339 =$

5 Write down the four number facts that connect the numbers below.

    400   152   248

Solving problems

A bus starts at Barnsley and makes four stops before reaching Penistone. At Barnsley 23 people get on. At Dodworth 12 people get off and 14 people get on. At Silkstone 15 people get off and 4 people get on. At Hoylandswaine 5 people get off and 6 people get on. At Cubley 9 people get off and 8 get on. At Penistone the rest of the passengers get off. How many people are on the bus?

When you solve problems, you need to develop a strategy: that is, a way to go about the problem. You also have to decide which mathematical operation you need to solve it. For example, is it addition, subtraction, multiplication or division or a combination of these? Something else you must do is to read the question fully before starting. The answer to the problem above is one! The driver.

Read the questions below carefully.

Exercise 3G

 1 It cost six people £15 to go to the cinema. How much would it cost two people?

2 There are 50 officers and 770 crew on board an aircraft carrier.

    a How many officers and crew are there on board altogether?

    b How many more crew members are there than officers?

    c 175 of the crew are female. How many of the crew are male?

FM **3** Ten pencils cost £4.50. How much would a hundred pencils cost?

4 If 135 + 44 = 179, write down, without calculating, the value of the following.

  a 179 – 44   **b** 179 – 135   **c** 235 + 44   **d** 135 + 544

5 If 260 – 155 = 105, write down, without calculating, the value of the following.

  a 105 + 155   **b** 260 – 105   **c** 260 – 55   **d** 560 – 205

6 Anthea has the following cards.

  a What is the largest number she can make with the cards?

  b What is the smallest number she can make with the cards?

7 Strips of paper are 40 cm long. They are stuck together with a 10 cm overlap.

  a How long would two strips glued together be?

  b How long would four strips glued together be?

FM **8** A can of Coke and a Kit-Kat together cost 80p. Two cans of Coke and a Kit-Kat together cost £1.30. How much would three cans of Coke and four Kit-Kats cost?

FM **9** A water tank holds 500 litres. How much has been used if there is 144 litres left in the tank?

10 Arrange the numbers 1, 2, 3 and 4 in each of these to make the problem correct.

  a ☐ + ☐ = ☐ + ☐   **b** ☐ × ☐ = ☐☐   **c** ☐☐ ÷ ☐ = ☐

Extension Work

Using the numbers 1, 2, 3 and 4 and any mathematical signs, make all of the numbers from 1 to 10.

For example: 2 × 3 – 4 – 1 = 1, 12 – 3 – 4 = 5

Once you have found all the numbers up to 10, can you find totals above 10?

3
I can solve real life problems using coins and currency.
I can add and subtract whole numbers.
I can remember simple multiplication facts.
I can solve problems involving whole numbers.

4
I can use and understand place value.
I can remember multiplication facts up to 10×10.
I can add and subtract decimals up to two decimal places.
I can multiply and divide whole numbers by 10 or 100.

5
I can estimate answers and check if an answer is about right.
I can multiply and divide decimals by 10, 100 and 1000.
I can add and subtract using negative and positive numbers.
I can tackle mathematical problems.

National Test questions

1 *2004 3–5 Paper 1*

There are **seven different ways** to make **8p** with coins.

Copy and complete the table to show the seven ways to make 8p.

Two have been done for you.

Number of 5p coins	Number of 2p coins	Number of 1p coins
0	0	8
0	1	6

2 *2004 3–5 Paper 1*

I have some **5p** coins and some **2p** coins.

I can use some of my coins to make **27p**.

5p coins   2p coins

a Copy and complete the table below to show different ways to make 27p.

The first way is done for you.

Ways to make 27p
Use five 5p coins and one 2p coin.
Use three 5p coins and ☐ 2p coins.
Use one 5p coin and ☐ 2p coins.

b I cannot make 27p from 5p coins and 2p coins using an **even** number of **5p coins**.

Explain why not.

3 *2006 3–5 Paper 1*

This number line shows one way to use **two steps** to move from 0 to 20.

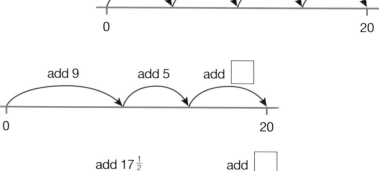

a On a number line like the one above, show a **different** way to use **two steps** to move from 0 to 20.

b The number line below shows how to use **four steps** of the **same size** to move from 0 to 20.

Complete the sentence:

   Each step is **add** …

c Find the missing number on each number line below to show how to move from 0 to 20.

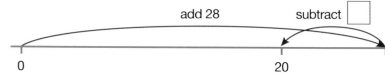

4 *2005 3–5 Paper 1*

a You can make six different numbers using these three digit cards: **3** **5** **7**

Complete the list to show the six different numbers.

b From the list, write down the **smallest** number and the **biggest** number, then add them together.

357
375

5 *2006 4–6 Paper 1*

Add three to the number on each number line.

The first one is done for you.

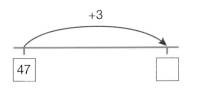 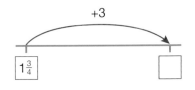 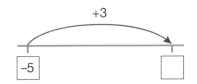

 6 *2005 4–6 Paper 2*

A meal in a restaurant costs the same for each person.

For **11** people the cost is **£253**.

What is the total cost for 12 people?

 7 *2003 Paper 1*

When the wind blows, it feels colder.

The stronger the wind, the colder it feels.

Fill in the gaps in the table.

The first row is done for you.

Wind strength	Temperature out of the wind (°C)	How much colder it feels in the wind (°C)	Temperature it feels in the wind (°C)
Moderate breeze	5	7 degrees colder	–2
Fresh breeze	–8	11 degrees colder	…
Strong breeze	–4	… degrees colder	–20
Gale	…	23 degrees colder	–45

 8 *2003 4–6 Paper 2*

The table shows how much it costs to go to a cinema.

Mrs Jones (aged 35), her daughter (aged 12), her son (aged 10) and a friend (aged 65) want to go to the cinema.

They are not sure whether to go before 6pm or after 6pm.

How much will they save if they go **after** 6pm?

Show your working.

	Before 6pm	After 6pm
Adult	£3.20	£4.90
Child (14 or under)	£2.50	£3.50
Senior Citizen (60 or over)	£2.95	£4.90

9 *2000 Paper 1*

Here is the 65 times table.

Use the 65 times table to help you work out 16×65.

Show how you did it.

10 *2001 Paper 1*

a In New York the temperature was –2 °C. In Atlanta the temperature was 7 °C warmer. What was the temperature in Atlanta?

b In Amsterdam the temperature was 3 °C. In Helsinki the temperature was –8 °C. How many degrees warmer was it in Amsterdam than in Helsinki?

```
1 × 65 = 65
2 × 65 = 130
3 × 65 = 195
4 × 65 = 260
5 × 65 = 325
6 × 65 = 390
7 × 65 = 455
8 × 65 = 520
9 × 65 = 585
10 × 65 = 650
```

This chapter is going to show you

- How to measure and draw lines
- How to find the perimeter and area of 2-D shapes
- How to draw a net for an open cube
- How to find the surface area of a cube

What you should already know

- Metric units of length
- Perimeter is the distance around the edge of a 2-D shape
- Area is the space inside a 2-D shape
- Names of 3-D shapes such as the cube and cuboid

Length, perimeter and area

Make sure that you know these:

10 mm = 1 cm
100 cm = 1 m
1000 m = 1 km

The unit of area used in this chapter is the square centimetre (cm²).

Example 4.1

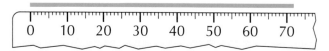

The length of this line is 6 cm.

Example 4.2

The length of this line is 72 mm or 7 cm 2 mm or 7.2 cm.

Remember: 1 cm = 10 mm.

Example 4.3

The side of each square on the grid is 1 cm.

The perimeter of the rectangle is the distance around its edge. So, here the perimeter is:

3 + 2 + 3 + 2 = 10 cm

Count the squares inside the rectangle to find its area.

So, the area of this rectangle is 6 cm².

Example 4.4

The side of each square on the grid is 1 cm.

The perimeter of the L-shape = 1 + 2 + 2 + 1 + 3 + 3
                                              = 12 cm

By counting the squares, the area of the L-shape = 5 cm².

Exercise 4A

1 Copy each of the following and write in the missing numbers.

    a   5 cm = _____ mm

    b   6.2 cm = 6 cm 2 mm = _____ mm

    c   7.5 cm = 7 cm _____ mm = _____ mm

    d   8.9 cm = _____ cm _____ mm = _____ mm

    e   _____ cm = _____ cm _____ mm = 94 mm

2 Measure the length of each of these lines.

    a

    b

    c

    d

    e

3 Measure the length of each of these lines. Give your answer in centimetres.

    a

    b

    c

    d

    e

4 Use your ruler to draw lines with the following lengths.

    a   4 cm   **b**   5 cm 4 mm   **c**   6.8 cm   **d**   7.1 cm   **e**   88 mm

5 The shapes are all regular polygons. Use your ruler to measure the perimeter of each one.

    a   **b**   **c**

Square

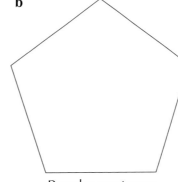

Regular pentagon

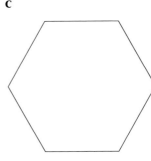

Regular hexagon

6 Copy these shapes onto 1 cm squared paper. Find the perimeter and area of each shape.

a

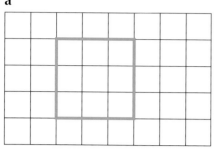

b

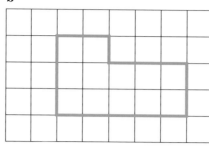

c

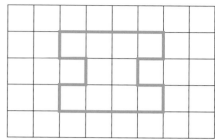

d

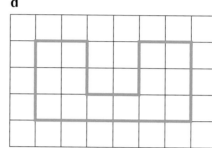

e

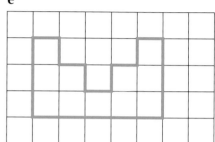

Extension Work

1 Use your ruler to measure the width of a 1p, a 2p, a 5p, a 10p and a £1 coin.

2 Working in pairs, you draw five lines. Then ask your partner to guess how long each line is. Then check the answers by measuring each one with a ruler.

3 Working in groups, draw the outline of each person's hand (or foot) on 1 cm squared paper. Estimate the area of each hand (or foot).

Make a display of all the hands (and/or feet) for your classroom.

Perimeter and area of rectangles

Length

Width

The perimeter of the rectangle is the total distance around the shape.

Perimeter = 2 lengths + 2 widths

Unit is mm, cm or m.

The area of the rectangle is the amount of space inside the shape.

Area = length × width

Unit is cm^2.

Example 4.8 ▷   Find the perimeter and area of each of the following.

a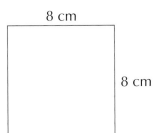

8 cm

8 cm

Perimeter = 8 + 8 + 8 + 8
               = 4 × 8
               = 32 cm

      Area = 8 × 8
            = 64 cm²

b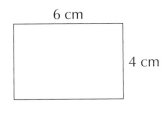

6 cm

4 cm

Perimeter = 6 + 6 + 4 + 4
               = 2 × 6 + 2 × 4
               = 12 + 8
               = 20 cm

      Area = 6 × 4
            = 24 cm²

Exercise 4B

(1) Find the perimeter of each rectangle.

a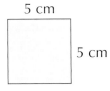
5 cm
5 cm

b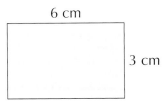
6 cm
3 cm

c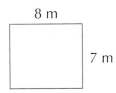
8 m
7 m

d
12 mm
15 mm

FM (2) (a) Find the perimeter of this room.

    (b) Skirting board is sold in 3 m lengths. How many lengths are needed to go around the four walls of the room?

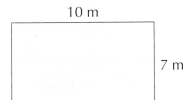
10 m
7 m

(3) A square tile measures 15 cm by 15 cm. Find the perimeter of the tile.

(4) A football pitch measures 100 m by 75 m. Find the perimeter of the pitch.

(5) Find the area of each rectangle.

a
4 cm
4 cm

b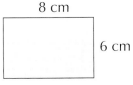
8 cm
6 cm

c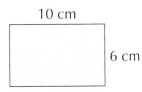
10 cm
6 cm

d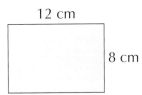
12 cm
8 cm

e
3 cm
3 cm

f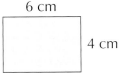
6 cm
4 cm

g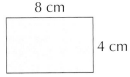
8 cm
4 cm

h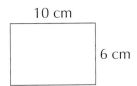
10 cm
6 cm

6 Draw a square with each side 6 cm. How many squares with each side 2 cm are needed to cover it?

7 Copy and complete the table for rectangles **a** to **f**.

	Length	Width	Perimeter	Area
a	4 cm	2 cm		
b	6 cm	5 cm		
c	8 cm	4 cm		
d	10 cm	9 cm		
e	8 cm	1 cm		
f	7 cm	2 cm		

Extension Work

1 On 1 cm squared paper, draw as many rectangles as you can with a perimeter of 20 cm.

2 On 1 cm squared paper, draw as many rectangles as you can with an area of 24 cm².

3 The shape on the right has a perimeter of 10 cm.

On 1 cm squared paper, how many more shapes can you draw with a perimeter of 10 cm?

3-D shapes

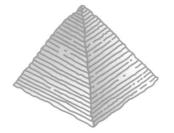

You should be able to recognise and name the following 3-D shapes or solids.

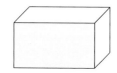

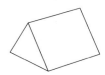

Cube   Cuboid   Square-based pyramid   Tetrahedron   Triangular prism

Example 4.6 The following 3-D shapes can be made from cubes.

a

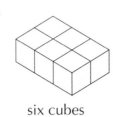

six cubes

b

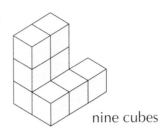

nine cubes

A **net** is a 2-D shape that is used to make a 3-D shape.

Example 4.7

This is a net which, when folded, will make an open cube like the one on the left. The shaded square of the net is at the bottom of the open cube.

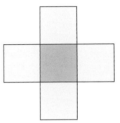

Exercise 4C

1 Find the number of cubes in each of the following 3-D shapes.

a

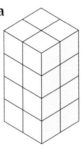

b

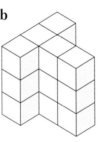

c

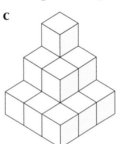

d

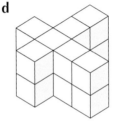

2 Each of these 3-D shapes below has been made using six cubes. There are three pairs of identical shapes. Write down the two letters of each pair which are identical.

a

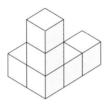

b

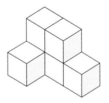

c

d

e

f

3 A cuboid has six faces, eight vertices and 12 edges.

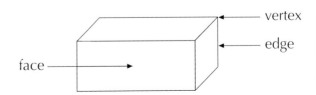

vertex

edge

face

How many faces, vertices and edges do each of these 3-D shapes have?

a 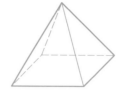 **b**  **c**

Square-based pyramid   Triangular prism   Tetrahedron

 On 1 cm squared paper, draw as many different nets as you can to make an open cube. You may need to cut them out to see if they fold up correctly. Shade the square that is at the bottom of the open cube.

Extension   Work

1   Draw a sketch of a net for each of the following 3-D shapes.
   a   cube   **b**   cuboid   **c**   square-based pyramid

2   **Euler's rule**
   Copy and complete the following table for six different 3-D shapes. Ask your teacher to show you these 3-D shapes.

Solid	Number of faces	Number of vertices	Number of edges
Cuboid			
Square-based pyramid			
Triangular prism			
Tetrahedron			
Hexagonal prism			
Octahedron			

Surface area of cubes

 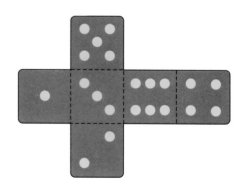

 The surface area of a cube is found by working out the total area of its six faces.

Example 4.8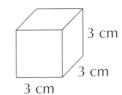

Find the surface area of this cube.

Area of one face of the cube $= 3 \times 3$

$= 9 \text{ cm}^2$

So, surface area of the whole cube $= 6 \times 9$

$= 54 \text{ cm}^2$

Exercise 4D

1 Find the surface area for each of the following cubes.

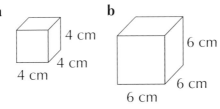
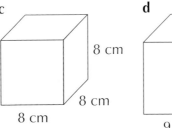
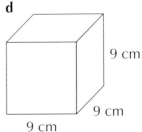

2 Find the surface area of this unit cube.

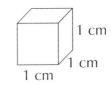

3 Find the surface area for each of the cubes with these edge lengths.

a 2 cm   b 5 cm   c 10 cm   d 12 cm

4 Find the surface area of the outside of this open box. (A cube without a top.)

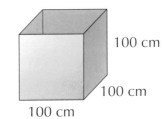

5 Six cubes are placed together to make these 3-D shapes.

a

b

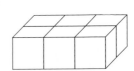

c

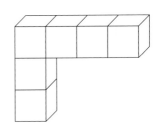

Find the surface area of each shape.

Extension Work

Cubes to cuboids

You will need 12 cubes for this activity.

All 12 cubes are arranged to form a cuboid.

How many different cuboids can you make?

3 I can draw and measure straight lines.

4 I can draw a net for an open cube.

I can find the perimeter of a 2-D shape.

I can find the area of a rectangle by counting squares.

I can make 3-D shapes from cubes.

5 I can find the area of a rectangle by using the formula Area = Length × Width.

I can find the surface area of cubes.

National Test questions

1 *2001 Paper 2*

a The diagram shows part of a ruler.

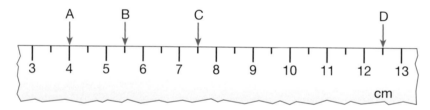

Complete these sentences.

The distance between A and B is …… cm.

The distance between C and D is …… cm.

b Look at the ruler below.

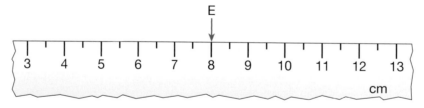

I want the distance between E and F to be $3\frac{1}{2}$ cm.

There are two places F could be. Show the two places by drawing arrows on a copy of the ruler.

2   *2000 3–5 Paper 2*

   a   What number is the arrow pointing to on this scale?

   b   Copy the scale below and draw an arrow on it to show the number **112**.

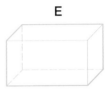

3   *2005 3–5 Paper 1*

Look at the diagrams showing 3-D shapes.

      A   B   C   D   E

   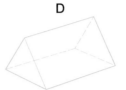

   a   One of the shapes has **one square face** and **four triangular faces**.

         Write the letter of this shape.

   b   Two of the shapes have **six faces**.

         Write the letters of these shapes.

   c   Now look at this diagram showing another 3-D shape.

         How many faces does the shape have?

4   *2000 Paper 2*

The shaded rectangle has an area of 4 cm^2
and a perimeter of 10 cm.

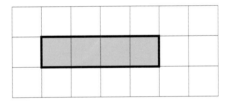

   a   Look at the cross-shape.

         The cross-shape has an area of ...... cm^2
         and a perimeter of ...... cm.

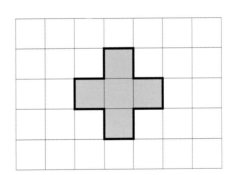

   b   Draw a shape with an area of 6 cm^2 on centimetre-squared paper.

   c   What is the perimeter of your shape?

4

FM 5 *2000 Paper 2*

Alika has a box of square tiles.

The tiles are three different sizes.

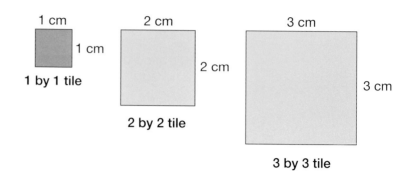

1 cm

1 cm

1 by 1 tile

2 cm

2 cm

2 by 2 tile

3 cm

3 cm

3 by 3 tile

She also has a mat that is 6 cm by 6 cm.

36 of the 1 by 1 tiles will cover the mat.

a How many of the 2 by 2 tiles will cover the mat?

b How many of the 3 by 3 tiles will cover the mat?

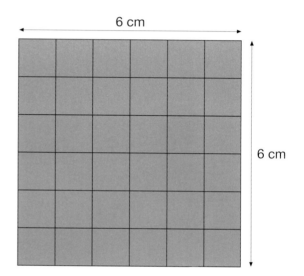

6 cm

6 cm

c Alika glues three tiles on her mat like this. Complete the gaps below.

She could cover the rest of the mat by using another two 3 by 3 tiles and another ...... 1 by 1 tiles.

She could cover the rest of the mat by using another two 2 by 2 tiles and another ...... 1 by 1 tiles.

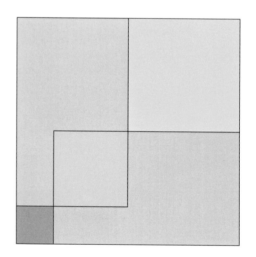

6 *2007 3–5 Paper 1*

The shape below is a regular pentagon.

All five sides are exactly the same length.

Measure accurately one of the sides, then work out the **perimeter** of the pentagon.

FM Design a bedroom

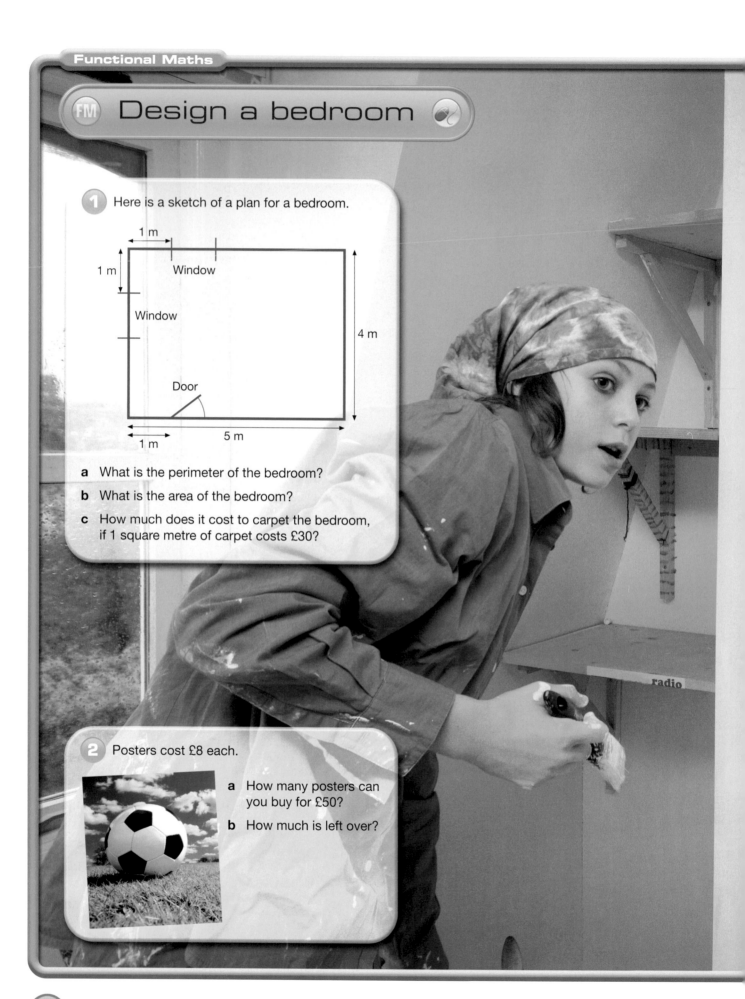

1. Here is a sketch of a plan for a bedroom.

   1 m

   1 m

   Window

   Window

   Door

   4 m

   5 m

   1 m

   a What is the perimeter of the bedroom?

   b What is the area of the bedroom?

   c How much does it cost to carpet the bedroom,
      if 1 square metre of carpet costs £30?

2. Posters cost £8 each.

   a How many posters can
      you buy for £50?

   b How much is left over?

radio

Use catalogues or the Internet to find how much it would cost to buy all the furniture for the bedroom.

3 Here are sketches of the door and one of the windows.

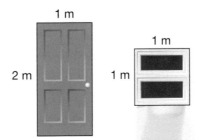

1 m

2 m

1 m

1 m

1 m

The height of the bedroom is 3 m.

a Find the area of each wall in the bedroom.

b What is the total area of all four walls?

c If a one-litre tin of paint covers 10 m², what is the smallest number of tins required to paint the walls?

Furniture challenge

4 Copy the plan of the bedroom onto centimetre-squared paper. Use a scale of 1 cm to $\frac{1}{2}$ m. Decide where you would put the following bedroom furniture. Use cut-outs to help.

Bed	Bedside table	Wardrobe	Chest of drawers	Desk
2 m by 1 m	$\frac{1}{2}$ m by $\frac{1}{2}$ m	$1\frac{1}{2}$ m by $\frac{1}{2}$ m	1 m by $\frac{1}{2}$ m	1 m by $\frac{1}{2}$ m

This chapter is going to show you	What you should already know
● How to extend your knowledge of fractions and percentages ● How to add simple fractions ● How to find equivalent fractions, percentages and decimals	● How to change an improper fraction into a mixed number ● How to use decimal notation for tenths and hundredths ● How to recognise simple equivalent fractions

Fractions

These diagrams show you five ways to split a 4 by 4 grid into quarters.

 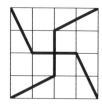 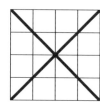 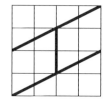 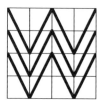

How many more different ways can you find to do this?

What about splitting the 4 × 4 grid into halves?

Example 5.1 ▷ Write down the fraction of each shape that is shaded.

a 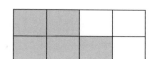 b 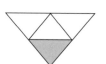 c

a $\frac{5}{8}$ The shape is divided into 8 equal parts (the denominator) and 5 parts are shaded (the numerator).

b $\frac{1}{4}$ The shape is divided into 4 equal parts (the denominator) and 1 part is shaded (the numerator).

c $\frac{5}{6}$ The shape is divided into 6 equal parts (the denominator) and 5 parts are shaded (the numerator).

Example 5.2 Fill in the missing number in each of these equivalent fractions.

a $\quad \dfrac{1}{3} = \dfrac{\square}{15}$
b $\quad \dfrac{5}{8} = \dfrac{\square}{32}$
c $\quad \dfrac{15}{27} = \dfrac{5}{\square}$

a Multiply by 5
b Multiply by 4
c Divide by 3

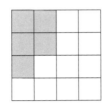
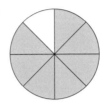
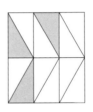

Exercise 5A

1 Write down the fraction of each shape that is shaded.

a
b
c
d

2 Draw a fraction diagram to show each fraction.

a $\quad \dfrac{1}{4}$
b $\quad \dfrac{2}{5}$
c $\quad \dfrac{3}{8}$
d $\quad \dfrac{1}{7}$

3 Copy and complete the following equivalent fraction series.

a $\quad \dfrac{1}{2} = \dfrac{2}{\cdots} = \dfrac{\cdots}{6} = \dfrac{8}{\cdots} = \dfrac{\cdots}{20} = \dfrac{\cdots}{150}$

b $\quad \dfrac{3}{4} = \dfrac{6}{\cdots} = \dfrac{\cdots}{12} = \dfrac{12}{\cdots} = \dfrac{\cdots}{40} = \dfrac{\cdots}{160}$

4 All of these fractions are equal to a half.

$$\dfrac{1}{2} = \dfrac{2}{4} = \dfrac{3}{6} = \dfrac{4}{8}$$

a What connects the top number (numerator) and the bottom number (denominator)?

b Make each of these fractions equivalent to $\frac{1}{2}$.

$$\dfrac{10}{\cdots} \quad \dfrac{6}{\cdots} \quad \dfrac{24}{\cdots} \quad \dfrac{8}{\cdots} \quad \dfrac{40}{\cdots} \quad \dfrac{11}{\cdots} \quad \dfrac{120}{\cdots} \quad \dfrac{\cdots}{10} \quad \dfrac{\cdots}{50} \quad \dfrac{\cdots}{14}$$

5 a All of these fractions are equal to $\frac{1}{3}$.

$$\dfrac{1}{3} = \dfrac{2}{6} = \dfrac{5}{15}$$

Make each of these fractions equivalent to $\frac{1}{3}$.

$$\dfrac{10}{\cdots} \quad \dfrac{4}{\cdots} \quad \dfrac{20}{\cdots} \quad \dfrac{8}{\cdots} \quad \dfrac{11}{\cdots} \quad \dfrac{13}{\cdots} \quad \dfrac{\cdots}{120} \quad \dfrac{\cdots}{24} \quad \dfrac{\cdots}{90} \quad \dfrac{\cdots}{9}$$

b All these fractions are equal to $\frac{1}{4}$.

$$\dfrac{1}{4} = \dfrac{2}{8} = \dfrac{5}{20}$$

Make each of these fractions equivalent to $\frac{1}{4}$.

$$\dfrac{10}{\cdots} \quad \dfrac{4}{\cdots} \quad \dfrac{20}{\cdots} \quad \dfrac{6}{\cdots} \quad \dfrac{\cdots}{100} \quad \dfrac{9}{\cdots} \quad \dfrac{\cdots}{44} \quad \dfrac{\cdots}{12} \quad \dfrac{\cdots}{20} \quad \dfrac{\cdots}{60}$$

6

$\frac{60}{300}$	$\frac{1}{5}$	$\frac{10}{20}$	$\frac{3}{15}$	$\frac{60}{240}$	$\frac{30}{90}$	$\frac{15}{45}$	$\frac{20}{100}$	$\frac{7}{21}$	$\frac{4}{20}$	$\frac{27}{54}$
$\frac{3}{9}$	$\frac{14}{42}$	$\frac{2}{10}$	$\frac{25}{75}$	$\frac{45}{90}$	$\frac{24}{48}$	$\frac{4}{8}$	$\frac{16}{32}$	$\frac{3}{12}$	$\frac{22}{88}$	$\frac{50}{100}$	$\frac{1}{4}$
$\frac{22}{44}$	$\frac{5}{15}$	$\frac{12}{48}$	$\frac{1}{3}$	$\frac{8}{24}$	$\frac{12}{60}$	$\frac{2}{8}$	$\frac{16}{80}$	$\frac{1}{2}$	$\frac{35}{70}$	$\frac{15}{60}$	$\frac{100}{400}$

Write down all the fractions in the box which are equivalent to:

a $\frac{1}{2}$ **b** $\frac{1}{3}$ **c** $\frac{1}{4}$ **d** $\frac{1}{5}$

7 Find the missing number in each of these equivalent fractions.

a $\frac{2}{3} = \frac{\square}{9}$ **b** $\frac{3}{8} = \frac{\square}{16}$ **c** $\frac{5}{9} = \frac{\square}{27}$

d $\frac{2}{5} = \frac{\square}{15}$ **e** $\frac{3}{7} = \frac{\square}{28}$ **f** $\frac{4}{9} = \frac{\square}{36}$

g $\frac{1}{5} = \frac{\square}{25}$ **h** $\frac{2}{11} = \frac{14}{\square}$ **i** $\frac{4}{9} = \frac{20}{\square}$

Extension **Work**

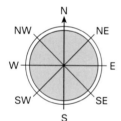

1 Clocks have 12 divisions round the face. What fraction of a full turn does:

a the minute hand turn through from 7:15 to 7:35?
b the minute hand turn through from 8:25 to 9:25?
c the hour hand turn through from 1:00 to 4:00?
d the hour hand turn through from 4:00 to 5:30?

2 This compass rose has eight divisions round its face. What fraction of a turn takes you from:

a NW to SW clockwise? **b** E to S anticlockwise?
c NE to S clockwise? **d** S to NE anticlockwise?
e W to SE clockwise? **f** N to NW clockwise?

Fractions and decimals

All of the grids below contain 100 squares. Some of the squares have been shaded in. In each case, write down the amount that has been shaded as a fraction out of 100 and as a decimal. What connections can you see between the equivalent values?

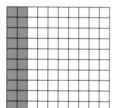 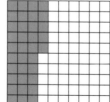  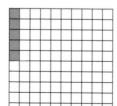  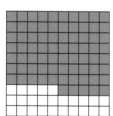

Example 5.3 Convert each of the following decimals to a fraction: **a** 0.6 **b** 0.04

a $0.6 = \frac{6}{10} = 6$ tenths **b** $0.04 = \frac{4}{100} = 4$ hundredths

Example 5.4 Convert each of these fractions to a decimal: **a** $\frac{3}{10}$ **b** $1\frac{7}{100}$

Use the column headings **T**ens, **U**nits, **t**enths, **h**undredths

a T U . t h
    0 . 3

b T U . t h
    1 . 0 7

Example 5.5 Write each of these as a fraction or decimal, as appropriate.

a 4.5 **b** 12.25 **c** $7\frac{3}{4}$

Three equivalent fractions and decimals that you should know are:

$\frac{1}{4} = 0.25$ $\frac{1}{2} = 0.5$ $\frac{3}{4} = 0.75$

So, the answers are:

a $4.5 = 4\frac{1}{2}$ **b** $12.25 = 12\frac{1}{4}$ **c** $7\frac{3}{4} = 7.75$

Exercise 5B

(1) Write each of these fractions as a decimal.

a $\frac{1}{10} =$ **b** $\frac{7}{10} =$ **c** $2\frac{1}{10} =$

d $2\frac{6}{10} =$ **e** nine tenths =   **f** four and seven tenths =

(2) Write each of these decimals as a fraction.

a 0.5   **b** 1.2   **c** 3.7   **d** 0.9   **e** 9.3   **f** 0.4

(3) Write each of these as a decimal.

a $\frac{7}{100}$ **b** $\frac{3}{100}$ **c** $2\frac{9}{100}$

d $2\frac{1}{100}$ **e** one hundredth =   **f** 4 and 5 hundredths =

(4) Write each of these as a fraction or a decimal, as appropriate.

a 6.5 =   **b** 7.5 =   **c** 1.5 =   **d** $8\frac{1}{2} =$ **e** $2\frac{1}{2} =$ **f** $11\frac{1}{2} =$

(5) Write each of these as a fraction or a decimal, as appropriate.

a 3.25 =   **b** 1.25 =   **c** 6.25 =   **d** $7\frac{1}{4} =$ **e** $2\frac{1}{4} =$ **f** $11\frac{1}{4} =$

(6) Write each of these as a fraction or a decimal, as appropriate.

a 1.75 =   **b** 6.75 =   **c** 4.75 =   **d** $5\frac{3}{4} =$ **e** $2\frac{3}{4} =$ **f** $3\frac{3}{4} =$

(7) Write each of these as a fraction.

a 0.8   **b** 2.2   **c** 3.7

d 5.2   **e** 0.06   **f** 9.1

5

8 Match each decimal to a fraction.

0.3	$\frac{9}{100}$	$\frac{8}{10}$	0.9	0.75	$\frac{8}{100}$	0.03	$\frac{9}{10}$	$\frac{4}{10}$
	0.08	$\frac{75}{100}$	0.8	$\frac{3}{10}$	0.4	0.09	$\frac{3}{100}$	

Extension Work

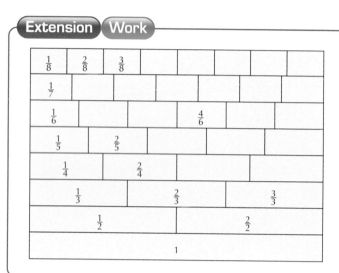

On squared paper outline an 8×8 grid.

Mark it off as shown. Then fill in the empty boxes with the rest of the values.

Use the diagram to put the correct sign ($<$, $>$ or $=$) between each pair of fractions.

a $\frac{2}{7} \ldots \frac{1}{5}$ **b** $\frac{3}{8} \ldots \frac{1}{3}$ **c** $\frac{3}{4} \ldots \frac{6}{8}$

d $\frac{1}{2} \ldots \frac{4}{7}$ **e** $\frac{2}{8} \ldots \frac{1}{4}$ **f** $\frac{3}{7} \ldots \frac{1}{3}$

g $\frac{3}{5} \ldots \frac{2}{3}$ **h** $\frac{1}{2} \ldots \frac{5}{8}$ **i** $\frac{5}{8} \ldots \frac{3}{5}$

j $\frac{3}{6} \ldots \frac{1}{2}$ **k** $\frac{5}{7} \ldots \frac{3}{4}$ **l** $\frac{2}{3} \ldots \frac{4}{6}$

Adding and subtracting fractions

Look at the fraction chart and the number line.

Explain how you could use them to show each of the following:

$\frac{1}{2} + \frac{1}{8} = \frac{5}{8}$

$1\frac{1}{2} + \frac{3}{8} = 1\frac{7}{8}$

$\frac{7}{8} - \frac{1}{4} = \frac{5}{8}$

$2\frac{1}{2} - \frac{5}{8} = 1\frac{7}{8}$

Example 5.6

a Use the number line to work out $\frac{5}{8} + \frac{1}{4}$.

b Use the fraction chart to work out $2\frac{1}{4} + 1\frac{3}{8}$.

a Start at $\frac{5}{8}$ and count on $\frac{1}{4}$ to take you to $\frac{7}{8}$.

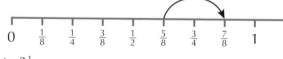

b Start at $2\frac{1}{4}$ on the fraction chart. Adding 1 takes you down one row to $3\frac{1}{4}$.

Counting on $\frac{3}{8}$ moves you three squares to the right. So the answer is $3\frac{5}{8}$.

Example 5.7

a Use the number line to work out $\frac{7}{8} - \frac{1}{2}$.

b Use the fraction chart to work out $2\frac{1}{4} - 1\frac{3}{8}$.

a Start at $\frac{7}{8}$ and count back $\frac{1}{2}$ to take you to $\frac{3}{8}$.

b Start at $2\frac{1}{4}$ on the fraction chart. Subtracting 1 takes you up one row to $1\frac{1}{4}$.

Counting back $\frac{3}{8}$ moves you from $1\frac{1}{4}$ to $1\frac{1}{8}$, then to 1, and then to $\frac{7}{8}$. So the answer is $\frac{7}{8}$.

Example 5.8

Work out each of the following: **a** $\frac{2}{5} + \frac{1}{5}$ **b** $\frac{3}{7} + \frac{5}{7}$ **c** $\frac{2}{9} + \frac{5}{9} - \frac{1}{9}$

Unless you can use a fraction chart or a number line, fractions must have the same denominator before they can be added or subtracted. The numerator of the answer is just the sum (or difference) of the original numerators. The denominator does not change. Sometimes it is possible to cancel the answer to its lowest terms.

a $\frac{2}{5} + \frac{1}{5} = \frac{3}{5}$ **b** $\frac{3}{7} + \frac{5}{7} = \frac{8}{7} = 1\frac{1}{7}$ **c** $\frac{2}{9} + \frac{5}{9} - \frac{1}{9} = \frac{6}{9} = \frac{2}{3}$

Example 5.9

Find the missing fraction: **a** $\frac{3}{13} + \ldots = 1$ **b** $3 - \frac{5}{9} = \ldots$

a $13 - 3 = 10$. So, $\frac{3}{13} + \frac{10}{13} = 1$.

b $9 - 5 = 4$. So, $3 - \frac{5}{9} = 2\frac{4}{9}$.

Example 5.10

a Change $\frac{17}{5}$ to a mixed number.

b Change $3\frac{2}{9}$ to a top-heavy fraction.

a $17 \div 5 = 3$ rem 2, so $\frac{17}{5} = 3\frac{2}{5}$.

b $3 \times 9 + 2 = 29$, so $3\frac{2}{9} = \frac{29}{9}$.

Exercise 5C

① Use the number line on page 62 to work out the following.

a $\frac{1}{8} + \frac{1}{8}$ **b** $\frac{1}{4} + \frac{1}{8}$ **c** $\frac{5}{8} + \frac{1}{2}$ **d** $\frac{1}{4} + \frac{7}{8}$

e $\frac{3}{8} + 1\frac{1}{8}$ **f** $\frac{5}{8} + \frac{3}{4}$ **g** $\frac{3}{8} + \frac{1}{2} + \frac{1}{4}$ **h** $\frac{7}{8} + \frac{3}{8} + \frac{1}{8}$

② Use the number line on page 62 to work out the following.

a $\frac{3}{8} - \frac{1}{8}$ **b** $\frac{1}{4} - \frac{1}{8}$ **c** $\frac{5}{8} - \frac{1}{2}$ **d** $1\frac{1}{4} - \frac{7}{8}$

e $1\frac{3}{8} - \frac{1}{8}$ **f** $1\frac{1}{2} - \frac{3}{4}$ **g** $\frac{3}{8} + \frac{1}{2} - \frac{1}{4}$ **h** $\frac{7}{8} - \frac{3}{8} - \frac{1}{8}$

③ Work out each of the following.

a $\frac{3}{7} + \frac{2}{7}$ **b** $\frac{1}{11} + \frac{4}{11}$ **c** $\frac{3}{5} + \frac{1}{5}$ **d** $\frac{7}{13} + \frac{3}{13}$

e $\frac{7}{11} - \frac{2}{11}$ **f** $\frac{4}{9} - \frac{2}{9}$ **g** $\frac{3}{7} - \frac{2}{7}$ **h** $\frac{3}{5} - \frac{1}{5}$

4 Complete each of these statements.

a

[grid] + [grid] = [grid]

$\frac{2}{3}$ + $\frac{1}{3}$ = ...

b

[grid] + [grid] = [grid]

$\frac{3}{5}$ + ... = 1

c $\frac{4}{7} + ... = 1$ **d** $\frac{5}{8} + ... = 1$ **e** $\frac{1}{10} + ... = 1$

f $\frac{5}{6} + ... = 1$ **g** $\frac{7}{12} + ... = 1$ **h** $\frac{13}{16} + ... = 1$

5 Complete each of these statements.

a $\frac{5}{12} + ... = 1$ **b** $\frac{5}{7} + ... = 1$ **c** $1\frac{1}{3} + ... = 2$

d $3\frac{1}{4} + \frac{3}{4} = ...$ **e** $2\frac{7}{8} + ... = 3$ **f** $2\frac{2}{5} + ... = 3$

g $1\frac{1}{8} + ... = 2$ **h** $2 - 1\frac{1}{4} = ...$ **i** $2 - 1\frac{1}{5} = ...$

j $3 - 2\frac{1}{4} = ...$ **k** $3 - 2\frac{1}{8} = ...$ **l** $2 - ... = \frac{1}{7}$

6 Change each of these top-heavy fractions into a mixed number.

a $\frac{9}{4}$ **b** $\frac{7}{3}$ **c** $\frac{5}{4}$

d $\frac{5}{3}$ **e** $\frac{8}{7}$ **f** $\frac{7}{2}$

g $\frac{10}{3}$ **h** $\frac{14}{3}$ **i** $\frac{14}{5}$

j $\frac{17}{6}$ **k** $\frac{17}{5}$ **l** $\frac{21}{5}$

7 Change each of these mixed numbers into a top-heavy fraction.

a $1\frac{3}{4}$ **b** $1\frac{4}{5}$ **c** $2\frac{2}{3}$

d $2\frac{3}{4}$ **e** $3\frac{1}{6}$ **f** $2\frac{3}{5}$

g $2\frac{1}{5}$ **h** $2\frac{1}{8}$ **i** $1\frac{7}{8}$

j $1\frac{1}{8}$ **k** $2\frac{1}{9}$ **l** $1\frac{2}{9}$

Extension Work

There are 360° in one full turn. 90° is $\frac{90°}{360°} = \frac{1}{4}$ of a full turn.

1 What fraction of a full turn is each of these?

a 60° **b** 20° **c** 180° **d** 30°

e 45° **f** 36° **g** 5° **h** 450°

2 How many degrees is: **a** $\frac{1}{8}$ of a full turn? **b** $\frac{1}{5}$ of a full turn?

3 360 was the number of days in a year according to the Ancient Egyptians. They also thought that numbers with lots of factors had magical properties. Find all the factors of 360.

4 Explain how the factors can be used to work out what fraction of a full turn is 40°.

Solving problems

Mrs Bountiful decided to give £10 000 to her grandchildren, nieces and nephews. She gave $\frac{1}{5}$ to her only grandson, $\frac{1}{8}$ to each of her two granddaughters, $\frac{1}{10}$ to each of her three nieces and $\frac{1}{20}$ to each of her four nephews. What was left she gave to charity. How much did they each receive? What **fraction** of the £10 000 did she give to charity?

The best way to do this problem is to work with amounts of money rather than fractions.

The grandson gets $\frac{1}{5}$ × £10 000 = £2000. Each granddaughter gets $\frac{1}{8}$ × £10 000 = £1250. Each niece gets $\frac{1}{10}$ × £10 000 = £1000. Each nephew gets $\frac{1}{20}$ × £10 000 = £500.

Altogether she gives away 2000 + 2 × (1250) + 3 × (1000) + 4 × (500) = £9500. This leaves £500. As a fraction of £10 000, this is $\frac{500}{10\,000} = \frac{1}{20}$.

Solve the problems in Exercise 5D. Show all your working and explain what you are doing.

Exercise 5D

1 Copy and complete each of these statements.

a $\frac{1}{10}$ of £60 = ...
b $\frac{3}{10}$ of £60 = ...
c $\frac{1}{10}$ of £50 = ...

d $\frac{7}{10}$ of £50 = ...
e $\frac{1}{10}$ of £10 = ...
f $\frac{5}{10}$ of £40 = ...

2 Copy and complete each of these statements.

a $\frac{1}{4}$ of £12 = ...
b $\frac{3}{4}$ of £12 = ...
c $\frac{1}{3}$ of £24 = ...

d $\frac{2}{3}$ of £24 = ...
e $\frac{1}{4}$ of £40 = ...
f $\frac{3}{5}$ of £50 = ...

FM **3** How many grams are there in $\frac{1}{2}$ of a kilogram?

FM **4** A school has 800 pupils. Three quarters of them get to school by bus. How many use the bus?

FM **5** A magazine has 240 pages. $\frac{2}{3}$ of them are used for adverts and the rest are articles. How many pages have articles on them?

6 Copy and complete these statements.

a   50% of £40 = ...
b   50% of £24 = ...

c   50% of £7 = ...
d   25% of 40p = ...

e   25% of £16 = ...
f   25% of £300 = ...

FM **7** A shop is taking 10% off all its prices. How much will these items cost after a 10% reduction?

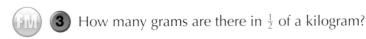 a Saucepan   £16.00
 b Spoon   60p

 c Coffee pot   £5.80
 d Bread maker   £54.00

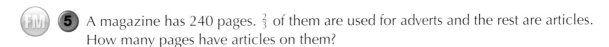 e Cutlery set   £27.40
 f Tea set   £20.80

8 Work out each of the following.

    a   Half of twenty-four   **b**   A third of thirty-six   **c**   A quarter of forty-four

    d   A sixth of eighteen   **e**   A fifth of thirty-five   **f**   An eighth of forty

9 Work out each of the following.

    a $\frac{2}{3}$ of 36 m   **b** $\frac{3}{4}$ of 44p   **c** $\frac{5}{6}$ of £18   **d** $\frac{4}{5}$ of 35 kg

    e $\frac{3}{8}$ of 40 cm   **f** $\frac{3}{7}$ of 42 km   **g** $\frac{4}{9}$ of 36 mm   **h** $\frac{5}{6}$ of £24

10 Calculate:

    a   10% of 240   **b**   35% of 460   **c**   60% of 150   **d**   40% of 32

    e   15% of 540   **f**   20% of 95   **g**   45% of 320   **h**   5% of 70

Extension **Work**

A spider diagram for 50 is shown using fractions and percentages.

Make up your own spider diagrams for different numbers.

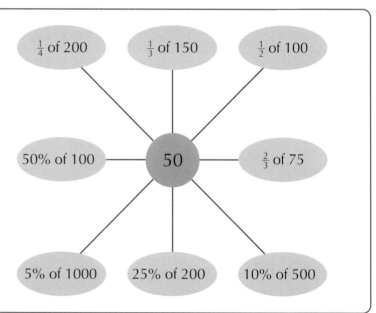

LEVEL BOOSTER

3   I can recognise and use simple fractions.

     I can recognise when two simple fractions are equivalent.

4   I can recognise approximate proportions of a whole.

     I can add and subtract simple fractions and those with the same denominator.

5   I can understand equivalent fractions, decimals and percentages.

     I can calculate fractions of a quantity.

     I can multiply a fraction by an integer.

1 *2004 3–5 Paper 1*

A shop sells sports equipment.

sports bag
£12.99

trampette
£17.99

basketball stand
£169

tennis raquet
£14.99

football
£5.99

a Mr Adams pays for a sports bag and a basketball stand.

Altogether, how much does he pay?

b Mrs Brown has £20. She pays for two footballs.

How much change should she get?

c Mrs Cooke has £50.

How many tennis rackets can she buy with £50?

 2 *2006 3–6 Paper 2*

A shop sells birthday cards.

Each card has a code that shows the price.

Code	Price of card
A	95p
B	£1.25
C	£1.65
D	£1.95
E	£2.35

a Karen pays for two cards.
One has code **A** on it; the other has code **C** on it.

Altogether, how much does Karen pay?

b Tariq pays for two cards.
Both cards have code **D** on them. He pays with a **£10** note.

How much change should Tariq get?

c Greg pays for two cards. Altogether he pays **£3.60**.

What could the **codes** on Greg's cards be?

There are two different answers. Write them both.

3 *2001 Paper 1*

a Copy the calculations and fill in the missing numbers.

$25\frac{1}{2} + \ldots = 27$

$150 - \ldots = 27$

$50\% \text{ of } \ldots = 27$

a quarter of $\ldots = 27$

b Write numbers to make each calculation correct.

$\ldots \times \ldots = 27$ $\qquad \ldots \div \ldots = 27$

4 *2001 Paper 2*

a Joe bought a box of cards for £6.80. He paid with a £10 note.

How much change should Joe get?

b Sanjay bought 15 boxes of cards. Each box cost £6.80.

How much did Sanjay pay for the boxes altogether?

c Amy paid £26.60 for some packets of cards. Each packet cost £1.90. How many packets did Amy buy?

5 *2005 4–6 Paper 1*

Here are four fractions.

$$\frac{3}{4} \qquad \frac{1}{8} \qquad \frac{1}{3} \qquad \frac{3}{5}$$

Look at the number line below.

Write the fractions missing from the boxes in the correct order from left to right.

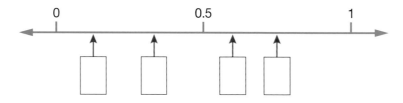

6 *2000 Paper 1*

A pupil recorded how much rain fell on five different days.

	Amount in cm
Monday	0.2
Tuesday	0.8
Wednesday	0.5
Thursday	0.25
Friday	0.05

a Copy the statements and fill in the gaps with the correct day

The most rain fell on ………………………..

The least rain fell on ………………………..

b How much more rain fell on Wednesday than on Thursday?

c How much rain fell altogether on Monday, Tuesday and Wednesday?

Now write your answer in millimetres.

7 *2001 Paper 1*

a Look at these fractions: $\frac{1}{2}$ $\frac{1}{3}$ $\frac{5}{6}$

Copy the number line and mark each fraction on it.

The first one has been done for you.

b Copy the fractions and fill in the missing numbers.

$$\frac{2}{12} = \frac{\square}{6} \qquad \frac{1}{2} = \frac{2}{\square} \qquad \frac{12}{\square} = \frac{6}{24}$$

8 *2006 3–5 Paper 1*

Write down the missing numbers:

$\frac{1}{2}$ of 20 = $\frac{1}{4}$ of $\square$ $\qquad$ $\frac{3}{4}$ of 100 = $\frac{1}{2}$ of $\square$ $\qquad$ $\frac{1}{3}$ of 60 = $\frac{2}{3}$ of $\square$

CHAPTER 6 Statistics 1

This chapter is going to show you

- How to calculate the mode and the range for a set of data
- How to interpret statistical diagrams and charts
- How to use the probability scale
- How to collect data from experiments and calculate probabilities

What you should already know

- How to interpret data from tables, graphs and charts
- How to draw line graphs, frequency tables and bar charts

Mode and range

Statistics is about how to collect and organise data. It also tells you how to interpret the data that you collect and present it in diagrams.

Often, you may not be provided with data and will have to collect it yourself. You might do this by asking a group of people questions and filling in a survey sheet, or by doing experiments and filling in an observation sheet.

Once you have collected data, you can organise it by putting it in a **frequency table**. The **frequency** is the number of times a particular value occurs in the data.

When interpreting data you will often need to find an **average**. The average is used in all sorts of everyday situations, because it represents a whole set of values by just a single, typical value. Some uses of averages that you might have heard of are: the average rainfall in Britain, the average score of a batsman, the average weekly wage, the average mark in an examination.

A common type of average that is easy to find is called the **mode**. (Other types of average will be met later.) The mode is the value that occurs most often in a set of data. Sometimes there may be no mode because either all the values in the data are different, or no single value occurs more often than other values.

The **range** of a set of values is the largest value minus the smallest value. A small range means that the values in the set of data are similar in size, whereas a large range means that the values differ considerably and therefore are more spread out.

Example 6.1 Here are the ages of 11 players in a football squad. Find the mode and range.

23 19 24 26 28 27 24 23 20 23 26

The mode is the number which occurs most often. So, the mode is 23.

The range is the largest number minus the smallest number: $28 - 19 = 9$. The range is 9.

Example 6.2 ▷ Below are the marks of 10 pupils in a mental arithmetic test. Find the mode and range.

19 18 16 15 13 14 20 19 18 15

There is no mode because no number occurs more often than the others.

The range is the largest number minus the smallest number: 20 – 13 = 7. The range is 7.

Exercise 6A

1 Find the mode of each of the following sets of data.

a   red, white, blue, red, white, blue, red, blue, white, red

b   rain, sun, cloud, fog, rain, sun, snow, cloud, snow, sun, rain, sun

c   E, A, I, U, E, O, I, E, A, E, A, O, I, U, E, I, E

d   ♠, ♣, ♥, ♦, ♣, ♠, ♥, ♣, ♦, ♥, ♣, ♥, ♦, ♥

2 Find the mode of each of the following sets of data.

a   7, 6, 2, 3, 1, 9, 5, 4, 8, 4, 5, 5

b   36, 34, 45, 28, 37, 40, 24, 27, 33, 31, 41, 34, 40, 34

c   14, 12, 18, 6, 10, 20, 16, 8, 13, 14, 13

d   99, 101, 107, 103, 109, 102, 105, 110, 100, 98, 101, 95, 104

3 Find the range of each of the following sets of data.

a   23, 37, 18, 23, 28, 19, 21, 25, 36

b   3, 1, 2, 3, 1, 0, 4, 2, 4, 2, 6, 5, 4, 5

c   51, 54, 27, 28, 38, 45, 39, 50

d   95, 101, 104, 92, 106, 100, 97, 101, 99

4 Find the mode and range of each set of data.

a   £2.50   £1.80   £3.65   £3.80   £4.20   £3.25   £1.80

b   23 kg, 18 kg, 22 kg, 31 kg, 29 kg, 31 kg

c   132 cm, 145 cm, 151cm, 132 cm, 140 cm, 142 cm

d   32°, 36°, 32°, 30°, 31°, 31°, 34°, 33°, 32°, 35°

5 A group of nine Year 7 pupils had their lunch in the school cafeteria. Given below is the amount that each of them spent.

£2.30   £2.20   £2.00   £2.50   £2.20
£2.90   £3.60   £2.20   £2.80

a   Find the mode for the data.

b   Find the range for the data.

6 The frequency table (right) shows the number of goals scored by a football team in their last 15 games.

Number of goals	0	1	2	3
Frequency	3	4	5	3

a   Write down the mode for the number of goals scored.

b   Find the range for the number of goals scored.

c   Draw a bar chart to illustrate the data.

When data has been grouped together into classes, as in the tally chart in Question 7, you may not know how often each individual value occurs. This means the mode cannot be found, but you can still find the **modal class**, which is the class with the most values in it.

7 Mr Kent draws a grouped frequency table to show the marks obtained by the 33 pupils in his science test.

Mark	Tally	Frequency
21–40	⦀⦀	
41–60	⦀⦀ ⦀⦀	
61–80	⦀⦀ ⦀⦀ I	
81–100	⦀⦀ I I	

   a Copy and complete the frequency column in the table.
   b Write down the modal class for Mr Kent's data.
   c What is the greatest range of marks possible for the data in the table?

8 **a** Write down a list of three numbers which have a mode of 10 and a range of 12.
   b Write down a list of four numbers which have a mode of 10 and a range of 10.
   c Write down a list of ten numbers which have a mode of 12 and a range of 8.

Reading data from tables and charts

Data is displayed in various forms, such as tables and charts. Exercise 6B will show you some of the different ways this can be done.

Exercise 6B

1 The calendar shows the dates of the days of the month of October in a certain year.

   a What day is 26 October?
   b What is the date of the second Sunday in the month?
   c A school's half-term holiday begins after 18 October and ends on 27 October. On how many days will Syed have to go to school in October?
   d On what day will 5 November fall in this year?

OCTOBER

M	Tu	W	Th	F	Sa	Su
		1	2	3	4	5	6
7	8	9	10	11	12	13
14	15	16	17	18	19	20
21	22	23	24	25	26	27
28	29	30	31			

2 The chart shows the distance, by road, in miles, between six cities in England.

Birmingham

121	**Leeds**				
120	198	**London**			
89	44	204	**Manchester**		
68	171	57	161	**Oxford**	
134	24	212	71	185	**York**

a How many miles is it from Leeds to London?

b How many miles is it from Birmingham to Oxford?

c Which two cities are the furthest apart?

d Frances drives from Manchester to Leeds. She then drives from Leeds to York. She then returns home from York to Manchester. How many miles has she driven altogether?

3 This two-way table shows the results of five football teams after 28 games.

	Games won	Games lost	Games drawn
Arsenal	16	5	7
Leicester City	3	17	8
Manchester United	18	7	3
Newcastle United	17	7	4
Southampton	10	14	4

a How many games did Newcastle United win?

b Which teams drew the same number of games?

c Three points are awarded for a win, one point is awarded for a draw and no points are awarded for a lost game.

  i How many points did Southampton get after the 28 games?

  ii Which team got the most points after 28 games?

  iii Which team got the least points after 28 games?

4 The line bar graph shows the marks in a mental arithmetic test for a class of Year 7 pupils.

a How many pupils got a mark of 6 in the test?

b How many pupils got a mark of 8 or more in the test?

c How many pupils are there in the class?

d Which mark is the mode?

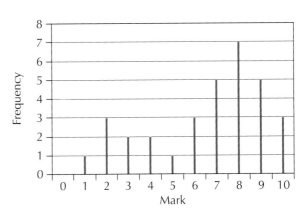

5 Phil throws a dice 30 times and obtains the following scores.

2	6	1	3	1	3	2	5	1	6
6	1	2	5	1	3	6	5	4	4
1	1	4	6	5	2	5	3	2	5

a Copy and complete the survey sheet below.

Score	Tally	Frequency
1		
2		
3		
4		
5		
6		
Total		

b Write down the mode for the scores.

c Write down the range for the scores.

d Draw a line bar graph for the data.

Average score

Throw a dice ten times. Record your results on a survey sheet. Draw a bar chart from your data.

Repeat the experiment but throw the dice 20 times. Draw another bar chart from your data.

Repeat the experiment but throw the dice 50 times. Draw a third bar chart from your data.

Write down anything you notice as you throw the dice more times.

Statistical diagrams

Once data has been collected from a survey, it can de displayed in various ways to make it easier to understand and interpret.

The most common ways to display data are to use pictograms, bar charts and line graphs.

Pictograms display data by using repeating symbols or pictures to show frequencies. The symbol or picture itself is usually worth a number of items. This is shown in a key.

Pictograms are often used in newspapers and magazines to attract attention more quickly.

Bar charts have several different forms. The questions in Exercise 6C will show you the different types of bar chart that can be used. Notice that data which has single categories gives a bar chart with gaps between the bars. Grouped data gives a bar chart with no gaps between the bars.

Line graphs are usually used to show trends and patterns in data.

Exercise 6C

1 The pictogram shows the amount of money collected for charity by different year groups in a school.

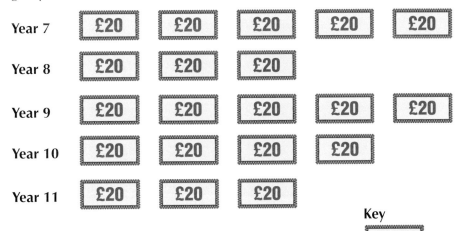

Key

£20 represents £20

a How much money was collected by Year 8?
b How much money was collected by Year 10?
c Which year group collected the most money?
d How much money was collected altogether?

2 The pictogram shows how many CDs five pupils have in their collection.

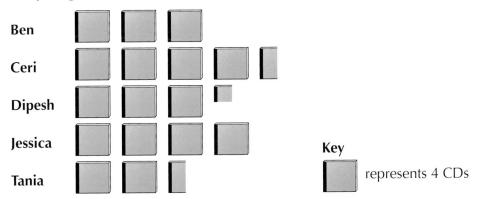

Key

represents 4 CDs

a Who has the most CDs?
b How many CDs does Jessica have?
c How many CDs does Ceri have?
d How many more CDs does Dipesh have than Tania?
e How many CDs do the five pupils have altogether?

3 The bar chart shows how the pupils in class 7PB travel to school.

a How many pupils cycle to school?
b What is the mode for the way the pupils travel to school?
c How many pupils are there in class 7PB?

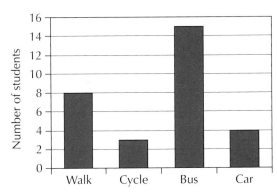

FM **4** The dual bar chart shows the daily average number of hours of sunshine in London and Edinburgh over a year.

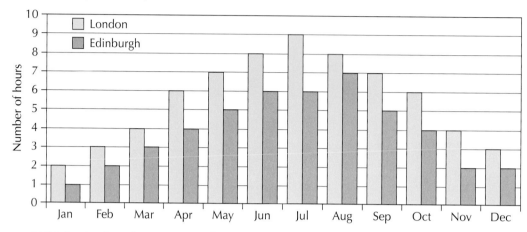

a Which city has the most sunshine?

b Which month is the sunniest for London and for Edinburgh?

c What is the range for the number of hours of sunshine over the year for London and for Edinburgh?

5 The percentage bar chart shows the favourite colours for a sample of Year 7 pupils.

a Which is the favourite colour of most pupils?

b What percentage of the pupils prefer yellow?

c Which two colours are equally preferred by the pupils?

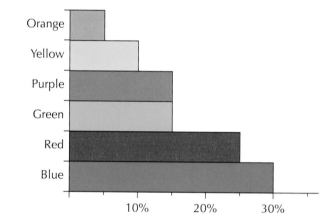

6 The bar chart shows the marks obtained in a mathematics test by the pupils in class 7KG.

a How many pupils are there in class 7KG?

b What is the modal class for the data?

c How many pupils got a mark over 60?

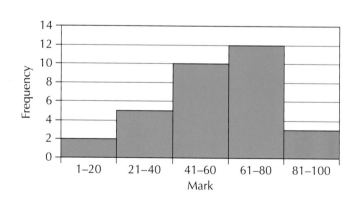

7 The line graph shows the average temperature, in °C, in Leeds over a 14-hour period.

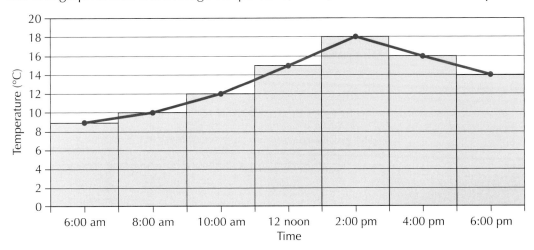

a What is the average temperature around 8 am?

b What is the average temperature at midday?

c Write down the range for the temperature over the 14-hour period.

Extension Work

Statistics in the press

Look through newspapers and magazines to find as many statistical diagrams as you can.

Make a display to show the variety of diagrams used in the press.

What types of diagram are most common?

How effective are the diagrams in showing the information?

Are any of the diagrams misleading? If they are, explain why.

Statistics in other areas

Do other subject areas in school make use of statistical diagrams?

Find examples in textbooks from other subjects to show where statistical diagrams are used most effectively.

Probability

Probability is the way of describing and measuring the chance or likelihood that an **event** will happen.

The chance of an event happening can be shown on a **probability scale**:

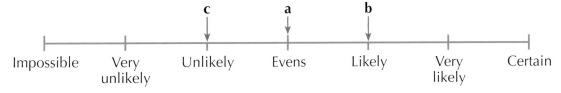

An evens chance is often referred to as 'a 50–50 chance'. Other everyday words used to describe probability are: uncertain, possible, probable, good chance, poor chance.

Example 6.3 ⬤ The following events are shown on the probability scale on page 79.

    a The probability that a new-born baby will be a girl.

    b The probability that a person is right-handed.

    c The probability that it will rain tomorrow.

To measure probability, we use a scale from 0 to 1. So probabilities are written as fractions or decimals, and sometimes as percentages, as in the weather forecast.

The probability scale is now drawn as:

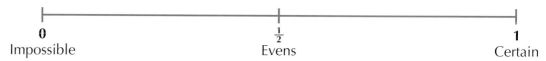

0	$\frac{1}{2}$	1
Impossible	Evens	Certain

Example 6.4 ⬤ A bag contains five counters. Two are red and three are blue.

When you take a counter out of the bag without looking, there are five to choose from and each one is equally likely to be taken. There are five **outcomes**, all **equally likely**.

The probability of choosing a red counter is 2 out of 5. This is written as:

    P(red) = $\frac{2}{5}$

Probabilities in examples like this one are usually written as fractions.

In the same way,

    P(blue) = $\frac{3}{5}$

The probability of choosing a green counter is:

    P(green) = $\frac{0}{5}$ = 0

since there are no green counters in the bag.

Example 6.5 ⬤ When tossing a fair coin, there are two possible outcomes: Head (H) or Tail (T).

Each outcome is **equally likely** to happen because it is a fair coin. So, the chance of getting a Head is the same as the chance of getting a Tail, which is $\frac{1}{2}$. This is written:

    P(H) = $\frac{1}{2}$ and P(T) = $\frac{1}{2}$

(Sometimes, people may say a 1 in 2 chance or a 50–50 chance).

Example 6.6 ⬤ When throwing a fair dice, there are six equally likely outcomes: 1, 2, 3, 4, 5, 6.

So, for example, the chance of throwing 6 is:

    P(6) = $\frac{1}{6}$

And the chance of thowing 1 or 2 is:

    P(1 or 2) = $\frac{2}{6}$ = $\frac{1}{3}$

Fractions are *always* cancelled down.

Exercise 6D

1 Choose one of the following words which best describes the probability for the events listed below.

impossible, very unlikely, unlikely, evens, likely, very likely, certain

a Manchester United will win their next home game.

b Someone in London will win the National Lottery this week.

c You have a maths lesson today.

d When throwing a dice, the score is an odd number.

e You will live to be 200.

f You will watch TV this evening.

g It will snow on Christmas Day this year.

2 The letters which make up the word

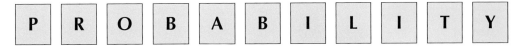

are put into a bag.

A letter is taken out of the bag. Write down, as a fraction, the probability that the letter is chosen is:

a T   **b** B   **c** I   **d** a vowel

3 Cards numbered 1 to 10 are placed in a box. A card is drawn at random from the box. Find the probability that the card drawn is:

a 5   **b** an even number   **c** a number in the 3 times table

d 4 or 8   **e** a number less than 12

4 A bag contains five red discs, three blue discs and two green discs. Linda takes out a disc at random. Find the probability that she takes out:

a a red disc   **b** a blue disc   **c** a green disc

d a yellow disc   **e** a red or blue disc

5 Mark is using a fair, eight-sided spinner in a game. Find the probability that the score he gets is:

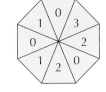

a 0   **b** 1   **c** 2   **d** 3

6 Mitchell has a box of coloured squares with shapes drawn on them.

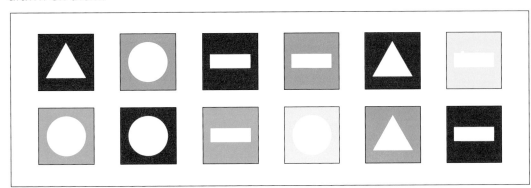

He takes out a square at random. Find the probability that he takes out:

a   a red square.

b   a square with a circle on it.

c   a green square with a triangle on it.

d   a blue square with a rectangle or a circle on it.

Extension Work

You will need a set of cards numbered 1 to 10 for this question.

Line up the cards, face down and in random order.

1   Turn over the first card.

2   Work out the probability that the second card will be higher than the first card.

3   Work out the probability that the second card will be lower than the first card.

4   Turn over the second card.

5   Work out the probability that the third card will be higher than the second card.

6   Work out the probability that the third card will be lower than the second card.

7   Carry on the process. Write down all your results clearly and explain any patterns that you notice.

Repeat the experiment. Are your results the same?

Experimental probability

Sometimes, a probability can be found only by carrying out a series of experiments and recording the results in a frequency table. The probability of the event can then be estimated from this result. A probability found in this way is known as an **experimental probability**.

To find an experimental probability, the experiment has to be repeated a number of times. Each separate experiment carried out is known as a **trial**.

The experimental probability can then be written as a fraction, as in the previous section.

Example 6.7   A dice is thrown 50 times. The results of the 50 trials are shown in a frequency table.

Score	1	2	3	4	5	6
Frequency	8	9	8	10	7	8

The experimental probability of getting $3 = \dfrac{8}{50} = \dfrac{4}{25}$.

Exercise 6E

1   Working in pairs, toss a coin 50 times and record your results in the following frequency table.

	Tally	Frequency
Head		
Tail		

a   Use your results to find the experimental probability of getting a Head.

b   What is the experimental probability of getting a Tail?

2 Working in pairs, throw a dice 100 times and record your results in the following frequency table.

Score	Tally	Frequency
1		
2		
3		
4		
5		
6		

a Find the experimental probability of getting 6.

b Find the experimental probability of getting an even score.

3 Working in pairs, drop a drawing pin 50 times.
Copy and record your results in the following frequency table.

	Tally	Frequency
Point up		
Point down		

a What is the experimental probability that the drawing pin will land point up?

b Is your answer greater or less than an evens chance?

Extension Work

Biased spinners

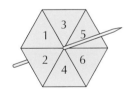

Make a six-sided spinner from card and a cocktail stick.

Weight it by sticking a small piece of Plasticine below one of the numbers on the card. This will make the spinner unfair or biased.

Spin the spinner 60 times and record the scores in a frequency table.

Find the experimental probability for each score.

Compare your results with what you would expect from a fair, six-sided spinner.

Repeat the experiment by making a spinner with a different number of sides.

3 I can read simple information charts.
I can read pictograms.

4 I can read bar charts and line graphs.
I can complete a tally chart.
I can find the mode of a list of data.
I can find simple probability.

National Test questions

1 *2005 Paper 1*

The table shows the average heights of boys and girls of different ages.

a What is the average height for **girls** aged **9 years old**?

b A boy and a girl are both **15 years old**.

Their heights are average for their age.

How much taller is the boy than the girl?

Age (years)	Average height for boys (cm)	Average height for girls (cm)
7	122	121
9	134	133
11	143	144
13	155	155
15	169	162

2 *2001 Paper 2*

The graph shows which pop stars had the most Number 1 singles in the UK charts.

Use the graph to answer these questions.

a How many Number 1 singles did George Michael have?

b Who had ten Number 1 singles?

c How many more Number 1 singles did Cliff Richard have than Take That?

d The graph shows that the Beatles and Elvis Presley came joint first. Cliff Richard came third. Who came joint fifth?

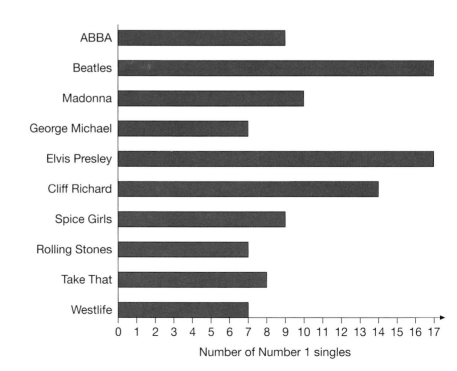

3 *2006 Paper 2*

Five people played each other at tennis.
The table shows who **won** each game.

For example, when Bob played Ann, Bob won.

	Ann				
Ann	✗	Bob			
Bob	Bob	✗	Carl		
Carl	Ann	Carl	✗	Dan	
Dan	Ann	Dan	Carl	✗	Ed
Ed	Ann	Bob	Carl	Dan	✗

a **Ann** played four games.

How many games did she win?

b Write the name of the person who **lost all** their games.

c Explain why there is a cross (✗) in some of the boxes.

4 *2005 Paper 1*

a There are two children in the Smith family.
The **range** of their ages is **exactly 7 years**.

What could the ages of the two children be? Give an example.

b There are two children in the Patel family. They are twins of the **same age**.

What is the **range** of their ages?

5 *2005 Paper 1*

a Jackie asked **27** people, 'Do you like school dinners?'
The bar chart below shows her results for 'Yes' and 'No'.

Copy and complete the bar chart to show her result for 'Don't know'.

b This pictogram also shows her results for 'Yes' and 'No'.

Copy and complete the pictogram to show her result for 'Don't know'.

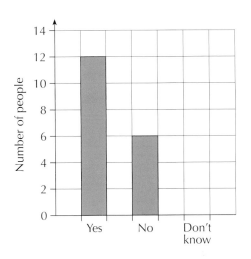

Yes	◯ ◯ ◯ ◯
No	◯ ◯
Don't Know	

6 *2007 Paper 2*

These are the names of the twelve people who work for a company.

Ali	Claire	Kiki	Suki
Brian	Claire	Lucy	Tom
Claire	James	Ryan	Tom

a What name is the mode?

b One person leaves the company. A different person joins the company.
Now the name that is the **mode** is **Tom**.

Complete the following sentences, writing in the missing names.

The name of the person who **leaves** is ......

The name of the person who **joins** is ......

School sports day

Teams

1 Ruskin team has seven members with the following ages:

	Age (years)
Joe	14
Kristen	15
Simon	13
Vikas	15
Helen	14
Sarah	13
Quinn	13

a Put these ages into order.

b What is the mode of the ages?

c What is the range of the ages?

100 m sprint

2 The girls' 100 m race was run in the following times:

	Time (seconds)
Kate	22
Kerry	25
Maria	21
Oi Yin	25
Sara	23

a Put these times into order.

b What is the mode of the times?

c What is the range of the times?

3 Alex had ten practice attempts at the long jump. The bar chart illustrates the range of lengths he jumps.

Range of jumps

He is now prepared for his last long jump.

a What range of lengths is Alex most likely to jump?

b What range of lengths is Alex least likely to jump?

Rounders competition

4 In the rounders game between Huntsman and Chantry, the following scorecards were produced as tallies. A tally was put next to a player each time they scored a rounder.

Huntsman		Frequency
Afzal	HHt	___
Claire	II	___
Gilbert	III	___
John	HHt II	___
Ali	I	___
Izolda	I	___
Kate	III	___
Joy	HHt HHt I	___
Mari	II	___

Chantry		Frequency
Ellen	IIII	___
Cynthia	II	___
Runuka	HHt I	___
Joanne	II	___
Michael	I	___
Emily	II	___
Julie	HHt II	___
Kay	HHt	___
Sue	III	___

a Copy and complete the frequency column for each team.

b Which team scored most rounders?

c Who won the game?

> **This chapter is going to show you**
> - How to use letters in place of numbers
> - How to use the rules (conventions) of algebra
> - How to solve puzzles called equations
> - How to solve problems using algebra

> **What you should already know**
> - Understand and be able to apply the rules of arithmetic

Finding unknown numbers

Part of algebra is finding **unknown numbers** in different sorts of problems.

Joy has 24 different shades of nail polish. Jess has 7 fewer than Joy. How many shades does Jess have?

Pete has 8 more marbles than Doug. They have 30 between them. How many marbles does Pete have?

These are examples of the types of problem that you will be solving by the end of the chapter.

Most of them can be thought of as simple puzzles, where you have to use arithmetic to work out the answer.

Example 7.1 ▷ In the two sums below, ☐ is a number. Find the number in each case.

   a ☐ + 4 = 10   **b** 7 + ☐ = 12

   a ☐ must be 6, since 6 + 4 = 10.

   b ☐ must be 5, since 7 + 5 = 12.

Note how ☐ represents a different number in each problem.

Any shape can be used to represent an unknown number, as shown in Example 7.2.

Example 7.2

Find the number represented by each shape.

a $\blacksquare \times 5 = 15$ **b** $9 - \blacklozenge = 2$

a $\blacksquare$ must be 3, since $3 \times 5 = 15$.

b $\blacklozenge$ must be 7, since $9 - 7 = 2$.

Exercise 7A

1 Copy and complete the following, replacing ☐ with a number to make each addition correct.

   a $6 + \boxed{} = 8$ **b** $5 + \boxed{} = 11$ **c** $2 + \boxed{} = 9$ **d** $7 + \boxed{} = 9$

   e $\boxed{} + 3 = 7$ **f** $\boxed{} + 5 = 8$ **g** $\boxed{} + 7 = 11$ **h** $\boxed{} + 4 = 9$

   i $1 + \boxed{} = 8$ **j** $\boxed{} + 8 = 12$ **k** $4 + \boxed{} = 10$ **l** $\boxed{} + 9 = 11$

2 Copy and complete the following, replacing ▼ with a number to make each multiplication correct.

   a $2 \times \blacktriangledown = 6$ **b** $5 \times \blacktriangledown = 10$ **c** $3 \times \blacktriangledown = 15$ **d** $4 \times \blacktriangledown = 12$

   e $\blacktriangledown \times 3 = 9$ **f** $\blacktriangledown \times 5 = 20$ **g** $\blacktriangledown \times 2 = 12$ **h** $\blacktriangledown \times 4 = 12$

   i $6 \times \blacktriangledown = 18$ **j** $\blacktriangledown \times 3 = 21$ **k** $8 \times \blacktriangledown = 24$ **l** $\blacktriangledown \times 5 = 30$

3 Copy and complete the following, replacing ★ with a number to make each subtraction correct.

   a $9 - \bigstar = 8$ **b** $10 - \bigstar = 7$ **c** $9 - \bigstar = 3$ **d** $12 - \bigstar = 5$

   e $\bigstar - 1 = 7$ **f** $\bigstar - 3 = 5$ **g** $\bigstar - 5 = 9$ **h** $\bigstar - 7 = 3$

   i $8 - \bigstar = 1$ **j** $\bigstar - 8 = 7$ **k** $15 - \bigstar = 11$ **l** $\bigstar - 8 = 4$

4 In each of these, state what number ♦ represents.

   a $8 + \blacklozenge = 11$ **b** $\blacklozenge + 5 = 8$ **c** $2 \times \blacklozenge = 10$ **d** $\blacklozenge \times 3 = 30$

   e $10 - \blacklozenge = 2$ **f** $\blacklozenge - 4 = 7$ **g** $\blacklozenge + 1 = 9$ **h** $9 - \blacklozenge = 3$

   i $5 \times \blacklozenge = 25$ **j** $8 + \blacklozenge = 13$ **k** $\blacklozenge \times 4 = 28$ **l** $\blacklozenge - 3 = 5$

5 In each sum below, find the number that the shape represents.

   a $\blacklozenge + 3 = 7$ **b** $7 - \bigstar = 2$ **c** $\blacktriangledown \times 4 = 16$ **d** $8 + \boxed{} = 9$

   e $\blacktriangledown + 7 = 12$ **f** $7 \times \blacklozenge = 14$ **g** $\boxed{} - 5 = 6$ **h** $6 \times \bigstar = 24$

   i $11 - \bigstar = 3$ **j** $\blacktriangledown \times 3 = 27$ **k** $9 \times \blacklozenge = 45$ **l** $\boxed{} \times 5 = 35$

Extension Work

See how many different correct answers you can find to these two puzzles.

a $5 + \blacklozenge + \blacktriangledown + \bigstar = 50$

b $100 - \blacklozenge - \blacktriangledown - \bigstar = 0$

Calculating using rules

Every day people use **rules** to make calculations connected with their jobs.

To use a rule, first you have to put known information into the rule. Then you make the calculation.

Example 7.3 ▷ Bill, the window cleaner, uses this rule to calculate how much he charges.

Charge = Number of Windows Cleaned multiplied by 40p

How much will Bill charge Marge for cleaning eight windows?

First, replace the Number of Windows with 8. The rule now becomes:

Charge = 8 × 40p

which is £3.20.

Exercise 7B

 1 The distance, in miles, travelled along a motorway can be calculated by the rule:

Distance = Number of Hours Driving multiplied by 70

How far did these people travel on a motorway?

a Angus, who travelled for 2 hours　　**b** Jenny, who travelled for 5 hours

 2 A rowing boat can be hired. The hire charge is found using the rule:

Hire Charge = Number of Hours multiplied by £2.50

How much will it cost to hire this rowing boat for the following times?

a 2 hours　　　**b** 3 hours　　　**c** 5 hours

 3 Mr and Mrs Mercer decide to give their three children monthly pocket money. They use the rule:

Pocket Money in Pounds = Child's Age plus 4

How much pocket money does each child receive a month?
Brian, aged 8　　Rachel, aged 13　　Gareth, aged 16

 4 The rule for calculating the area of a rectangle is:

Area = Length multiplied by Width

Calculate the area of each of these rectangles.

a Length 5 cm, width 3 cm　　　　　**a** Length 7 cm, width 6 cm

 5 The perimeter of a circle can be estimated by the following rule:

Perimeter is approximately three times the distance across the circle

Estimate the perimeter of each of these circles.

a 5 cm across　　**b** 8 cm across　　**c** 11 m across

6 The average speed of a journey is found by the rule:

Average Speed = Miles divided by Hours

Find the average speed for these journeys.
  a Karen travelled 100 miles in 2 hours.
  b Ahmed travelled 200 miles in 5 hours.
  c Wellington travelled 400 miles in 8 hours.

 7 Large potatoes are cooked in the microwave for the number of minutes calculated with the following rule:

Cooking Time = Seven multiplied by the Number of Potatoes, then add 3

Calculate the time needed to cook:
  a 1 potato   **b** 2 potatoes   **c** 3 potatoes

 8 A DJ charges for discos using the rule:

Charge = £50 plus £30 for every extra hour past midnight

How much would the DJ charge for the following discos?
  a Finish at 1:00 am   **b** Finish at 3:00 am

Extension   Work

- Think of a number between 1 and 9.
- Multiply this number by 9.
- Add 1.
- Add together the digits of your answer.
- Divide the result by 2.
- Find which letter matches your number from:
    1 → A   2 → B   3 → C   4 → D
    5 → E   6 → F   7 → G   8 → H
- Write down an animal beginning with that letter.

Try this out with a few different starting numbers. What do you notice?

Algebraic terms and expressions

In algebra, you will keep meeting three words: **variable**, **term** and **expression**.

Variable. This is the letter in a term or an expression whose value can vary. Some of the letters most used for variables are x, y, n and t.

Term. This is an algebraic quantity which contains only letters and may contain a number. For example:

$3n$ means 3 multiplied by the variable n

$\frac{n}{2}$ means n divided by 2

Expression. This is a combination of letters (variables) and signs, often with numbers. For example:

$8 - n$ means subtract n from 8
$n - 3$ means subtract 3 from n
$2n + 1$ means n multiplied by 2, then add 1

When you give a particular value to the variable in an expression, the expression takes on a particular value.

For example, if the variable n takes the value of 4, then the terms and expressions which include this variable will have particular values, as shown below:

$3n = 12$ because $3 \times 4 = 12$ $\frac{n}{2} = 2$ because $\frac{4}{2} = 2$

$8 - n = 4$ because $8 - 4 = 4$ $n - 3 = 1$ because $4 - 3 = 1$

Exercise 7C

(1) Write terms, or expressions, to illustrate the following sentences.

a	Add four to n.	**b** Multiply n by eight.	**c** Nine minus n.
d	Multiply t by 3.	**e** Divide t by five.	**f** Subtract t from seven.
g	Multiply x by three.	**h** Multiply six by x.	
i	Multiply y by five.	**j** Multiply 7 by y.	

(2) Write down the values of each expression for the three values of n.

a	$n + 1$	where	**i**	$n = 2$	**ii**	$n = 5$	**iii**	$n = 11$
b	$n + 5$	where	**i**	$n = 6$	**ii**	$n = 14$	**iii**	$n = 8$
c	$n + 7$	where	**i**	$n = 3$	**ii**	$n = 6$	**iii**	$n = 7$
d	$n + 2$	where	**i**	$n = 7$	**ii**	$n = 5$	**iii**	$n = 9$
e	$n - 3$	where	**i**	$n = 10$	**ii**	$n = 5$	**iii**	$n = 20$
f	$n - 1$	where	**i**	$n = 5$	**ii**	$n = 4$	**iii**	$n = 8$
g	$n - 4$	where	**i**	$n = 20$	**ii**	$n = 50$	**iii**	$n = 100$

(3) Write down the values of each expression for the three values of t.

a	$3t$	where	**i**	$t = 3$	**ii**	$t = 4$	**iii**	$t = 12$
b	$5t$	where	**i**	$t = 8$	**ii**	$t = 14$	**iii**	$t = 11$
c	$2t$	where	**i**	$t = 4$	**ii**	$t = 7$	**iii**	$t = 1$
d	$10t$	where	**i**	$t = 2$	**ii**	$t = 5$	**iii**	$t = 7$
e	$4t$	where	**i**	$t = 3$	**ii**	$t = 4$	**iii**	$t = 8$
f	$6t$	where	**i**	$t = 1$	**ii**	$t = 5$	**iii**	$t = 9$
g	$9t$	where	**i**	$t = 4$	**ii**	$t = 3$	**iii**	$t = 7$

(4) Write down the values of each expression for the three values of n or t.

a	$3 + n$	where	**i**	$n = 2$	**ii**	$n = 3$	**iii**	$n = 4$
b	$8 + t$	where	**i**	$t = 5$	**ii**	$t = 6$	**iii**	$t = 7$
c	$10 - t$	where	**i**	$t = 8$	**ii**	$t = 9$	**iii**	$t = 10$
d	$20 - t$	where	**i**	$t = 5$	**ii**	$t = 4$	**iii**	$t = 3$
e	$15 - n$	where	**i**	$n = 4$	**ii**	$n = 5$	**iii**	$n = 6$

Write down the values of each expression for the three values of n.

1 $2n + 3$ where **a** $n = 2$ **b** $n = 5$ **c** $n = 7$

2 $5n - 1$ where **a** $n = 3$ **b** $n = 4$ **c** $= 8$

3 $20 - 2n$ where **a** $n = 1$ **b** $n = 5$ **c** $n = 9$

4 $n^2 - 1$ where **a** $n = 2$ **b** $n = 3$ **c** $n = 4$

5 $5 + n^2$ where **a** $n = 8$ **b** $n = 9$ **c** $n = 10$

6 $n^2 + 9$ where **a** $n = 5$ **b** $n = 4$ **c** $n = 3$

Simplifying expressions

If you add 2 cups to 3 cups, you get 5 cups.
In algebra, this can be represented as:

$$2c + 3c = 5c$$

The terms here are called **like terms**, because they are all multiples of c.

Only like terms can be added or subtracted to simply an expression. Unlike terms cannot be combined.

Check out these two boxes.

Examples of combining like terms

$3p + 4p = 7p$ $5t + 3t = 8t$

$9w - 4w = 5w$ $12q - 5q = 7q$

$a + 3a + 7a = 11a$

$15m - 2m - m = 12m$

Examples of unlike terms

$x + y$ $2m + 3p$

$7 - 3y$ $5g + 2k$

$m - 3p$

Like terms can be combined even when they are mixed together with unlike terms.
For example:

2 apples and 1 pear added to 4 apples and 2 kiwis make 6 apples, 1 pear and 2 kiwis, or in algebra:

$$2a + p + 4a + 2k = 6a + 2k + p$$

Examples of different sorts of like terms mixed together

$4t + 5m + 2m + 3t + m = 7t + 8m$

$5k + 4g - 2k - g = 3k + 3g$

NOTE: You **never** write the one in front of a variable.

$g = 1g$ $m = 1m$

Example 7.4 ▷ Expand $3(a + 5)$.

This means that each term in the brackets is multiplied by the number outside the brackets. This gives:

$$3 \times a + 3 \times 5 = 3a + 15$$

Example 7.5 ▷ Expand and simplify $2(3p + 4) + 3(4p + 1)$.

This means that each term in each pair of brackets is multiplied by the number outside the brackets. This gives:

$$2 \times 3p + 2 \times 4 + 3 \times 4p + 3 \times 1$$
$$= 6p + 8 + 12p + 3$$
$$= 18p + 11$$

Exercise 7D

(1) Simplify each of the following expressions.

a $4c + 2c$	**b** $6d + 4d$	**c** $7p - 5p$	**d** $2x + 5x + 3x$
e $4t + 2t - t$	**f** $7m - 3m$	**g** $q + 5q - 2q$	**h** $a + 6a - 3a$
i $4p + p - 2p$	**j** $2w + 3w - w$	**k** $4t + 3t - 5t$	**l** $5g - g - 2g$

(2) Simplify each of the following expressions.

a $2x + 2y + 3x + 3y$	**b** $4w + 6t - 2w - 2t$	**c** $4m + 7n + 3m - n$
d $4x + 8y - 2y - 3x$	**e** $8 + 4x - 3 + 2x$	**f** $8p + 9 - 3p - 4$
g $2y + 4x - 3 + x - y$	**h** $5d + 8c - 4c + 7$	**i** $4f + 2 + 3d - 1 - 3f$
j $8c + 7 - 7c - 4$	**k** $2p + q + 3p - q$	**l** $3t + 9 - t$

(3) Simplify each of the following expressions if possible (3 of them will not simplify).

a $3n + 5 + 5n - 6$	**b** $5c + 4d - c + 7d$	**c** $6f - 5g + 2f + 7g$
d $n + 3 + 5m - 6p$	**e** $2x + 5y + x - 8y$	**f** $3m + 4p - 6m + 9p$
g $2t + 5 - 7p - 6s$	**h** $8x + 4y - 4x + 6y$	**i** $8r + 5s - 6r - 7s$
j $8t + 5s - 5t - 6s$	**k** $2c + 3d - 3e + 6f$	**l** $9x + 5x + 2x + 7y$

(4) Simplify each of the following expressions.

a $4x + 5 + 5x - 5$	**b** $3n + 4m - 3n + 7m$	**c** $6x - 5y + 2x + 5y$
d $2n + 7 + 5n - 7$	**e** $6a + 5b - 6a - 8b$	**f** $7m - 2p - 5m + 2p$
g $8t - 1 - 7t + 1$	**h** $2x - 4y - 2x + 4y$	**i** $6r + 2s - 6r - 4s$

(5) a What did you notice about all of the problems in question 4?

    b Simplify each of these expressions.

i $2x + 9 + 2x - 9$	**ii** $7x + 8y - 7x + 5y$	**iii** $7x - y + 5x + y$
iv $9x + 1 + 7x - 1$	**v** $4x + 9y - 4x - 9y$	**vi** $x - y - x + y$

A three-tier set of bricks looks like this:

The expressions on two bricks next to each other are added to give the expression on the brick above them.

Find the top brick expression when the bottom bricks, in order, are:

a $a + b$, $2a + 2b$ and $a + 3b$

b $2a + 1$, $3a - 2$ and $4a + 5$

c $3a + 2b$, $a - b$ and $2a + 3b$

(brick diagram: top $9a$; middle $3a$, $6a$; bottom a, $2a$, $4a$)

Equations

An equation states that two things are equal. These can be two expressions or an expression and a quantity.

An equation can be represented by a pair of scales.

When the scales balance, both sides are equal.

The left-hand pan has 3 bags each containing the same number of marbles.

The right-hand pan has 15 marbles.

How many marbles are there in each bag?

Let the number of marbles in each bag be x, which gives $3x = 15$

Divide both sides by 3: $\dfrac{3x}{3} = \dfrac{15}{3}$

There are 5 marbles in each bag. $x = 5$

Simple equations are solved by adding, subtracting, multiplying or dividing each side to find the value of x.

Example 7.6 Solve $x + 5 = 9$.

Subtract 5 from both sides: $x + 5 - 5 = 9 - 5$
$$x = 4$$

Example 7.7 Solve $\dfrac{x}{3} = 5$.

Multiply both sides by 3: $x = 3 \times 5$
$$x = 15$$

Exercise 7E

1 Solve each of these equations.

a	$2x = 10$	**b**	$3x = 18$	**c**	$5x = 15$	**d**	$4x = 8$
e	$3m = 12$	**f**	$5m = 30$	**g**	$7m = 14$	**h**	$4m = 20$
i	$6k = 12$	**j**	$5k = 25$	**k**	$3k = 27$	**l**	$2k = 16$
m	$7x = 21$	**n**	$4x = 28$	**o**	$5x = 40$	**p**	$9x = 54$

2 Solve each of these equations.

a	$x + 2 = 7$	**b**	$x + 3 = 9$	**c**	$x + 8 = 10$	**d**	$x + 1 = 5$
e	$m + 3 = 7$	**f**	$m - 3 = 5$	**g**	$k - 2 = 9$	**h**	$p - 5 = 9$
i	$k + 7 = 15$	**j**	$k - 1 = 3$	**k**	$m + 3 = 9$	**l**	$x - 3 = 7$
m	$x + 8 = 9$	**n**	$n - 2 = 6$	**o**	$m - 5 = 8$	**p**	$x + 12 = 23$

3 Solve each of the following equations.

a	$\frac{x}{2} = 5$	**b**	$\frac{x}{4} = 7$	**c**	$\frac{x}{3} = 11$	**d**	$\frac{x}{5} = 6$
e	$\frac{x}{4} = 8$	**f**	$\frac{x}{2} = 6$	**g**	$\frac{x}{8} = 3$	**h**	$\frac{x}{9} = 10$
i	$\frac{x}{3} = 11$	**j**	$\frac{x}{7} = 3$	**k**	$\frac{x}{5} = 9$	**l**	$\frac{x}{2} = 16$
m	$\frac{x}{10} = 3$	**n**	$\frac{x}{8} = 8$	**o**	$\frac{x}{2} = 20$	**p**	$\frac{x}{9} = 9$

Extension Work

The solution to each of these equations is a whole number between 1 and 9 inclusive.

Try to find the value.

a	$2x + 3 = 11$	**b**	$3x + 4 = 10$	**c**	$5x - 1 = 29$	**d**	$4x - 3 = 25$
e	$3m - 2 = 13$	**f**	$5m + 4 = 49$	**g**	$7m + 3 = 24$	**h**	$4m - 5 = 23$
i	$6k + 1 = 25$	**j**	$5k - 3 = 2$	**k**	$3k - 1 = 23$	**l**	$2k + 5 = 15$
m	$7x - 3 = 18$	**n**	$5x + 3 = 43$	**o**	$5x + 6 = 31$	**p**	$9x - 4 = 68$

LEVEL BOOSTER

3 I can find missing numbers represented by a symbol in simple problems such as
♦ + 3 = 7 and 3 × ■ = 15.

I can write a simple algebraic expression for a rule such as 4 more than x, e.g. $x + 4$.

4 I can substitute numbers into algebraic expressions such as $n + 3$, e.g. when $n = 5$, $2n + 3 = 13$.

I can simplify algebraic expressions such as $2a + 5a$ by collecting like terms, e.g. $7a$.

I can substitute into and use formulae in words describing real life situations such as the cost of a taxi fare as 'Cost = the numbers of miles times three', which is £15 when the journey is 5 miles.

I can solve simple equations involving one operation such as $2x = 12$, giving $x = 6$.

5 I can simplify algebraic expressions such as $2a + 5b + 3a - 2b$ by collecting like terms,
e.g. $5a + 3b$.

1   *2004 3–5 Paper 2*

Work out the values of a, b and c in the number sentences below:

$3 \times 10 + 4 = a$

$3 \times 10 + b = 38$

$c \times 10 + 12 = 52$

2   *2003 3–5 Paper 2*

I have two bags of cubes.

Each bag contains more than 20 but fewer than 30 cubes.

a   I can **share** the cubes in bag A **equally between 9** people.

How many cubes are in bag A?

b   I can **share** the cubes in bag B **equally between 4** people.

How many cubes could be in bag B?

There are two answers. Write them both.

3   *2003 3–5 Paper 1*

Simplify these expressions:

$5k + 7 + 3k = \boxed{}$ $k + 1 + k + 4 = \boxed{}$

4   *2005 3–5 Paper 2*

Look at this algebra grid:

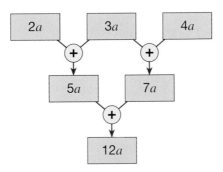

Copy and complete the algebra grids below, simplifying each expression.

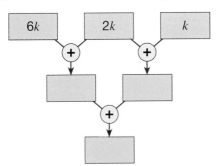
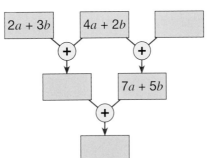

Skiing trip

Use the information in the key to answer the following questions.

Ski Hire Prices

ADULTS	Public price	Online price
Platinum Saloman Crossmax W12 – or equivalent	€240.70	€192.56
Gold Rossignol Radical 8S ou 8X Oversize – or equivalent	€214.90	€171.92
Silver Saloman Aero RT – or equivalent	€173.00	€138.40
Bronze Ski Bronze – or equivalent	€122.20	€97.76
CHILDREN	Public price	Online price
Junior Surf Dynastar Starlett Teen – or equivalent	€122.20	€97.76
Junior Ski Saloman X-wing fury Junior– or equivalent	€74.30	€59.44
Kid Dynastar My First Dynastar – or equivalent	€66.90	€44.72

1 If you order online it is cheaper than the normal 'public' price.

How much cheaper are the following online than normal?

a Adult 'Platinum' deal

b Adult 'Silver' deal

c Children's 'Junior surf' deal

2 Mr Khan, Mrs Khan, their son Rafiq and their daughter Sufia hire skis online.

Mr Khan hires a pair of Saloman Crossmax W12, Mrs Khan hires a pair of Saloman Aero RT, Rafiq hires a pair of Dynastar Starlett Teen and Sufia hires a pair of Saloman X-wing Fury Junior. What is their total bill?

3 The hire company allows a €20 discount per person for groups of 8 or more people. A party of 12 friends take a skiing trip. They all go for the Adult 'Platinum' deal and book online.

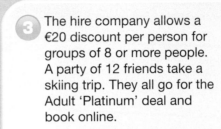

a What is the cost of this deal for one person with the discount?

b How much will the 12 friends pay altogether?

4 Mr Smith hires some Saloman Crossmax W12 skis online. He pays £20 as a deposit. The exchange rate is £1 = €1.38. How many more Euros will he have to pay?

5 Colne Valley High School take a party skiing. The bill for ski hire, which was booked online, is shown below. Complete the bill.

Invoice for Colne Valley

Number of rentals	Type of ski	Total cost
11	Junior Surf	
9	Junior Ski	
10	Kid	
3	Platinum	
2	Gold	
	Total hire cost	
	Less 10% discount	
	Total less discount	

This chapter is going to show you	What you should already know
• The vocabulary and notation for lines and angles • How to use angles at a point and angles on a straight line • How to use coordinates	• The geometric properties of triangles and quadrilaterals • How to plot coordinates

Lines and angles

Lines

A **line segment** has a fixed length.

A ——————————————————— B

The line segment AB has two end points, one at A and the other at B.

Two lines are either parallel or intersect.

   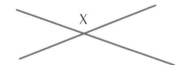   

Parallel lines never meet.   These two lines **intersect** at a point X.   These two lines intersect at right angles. We say the lines are **perpendicular**.

Angles

When two lines meet at a point, they form an **angle**. An angle is a measure of rotation and is measured in degrees (°).

Compass points

A compass shows the four main directions: North, East, South and West. You can use a compass to find the amount of turn you need to get from one direction to another.

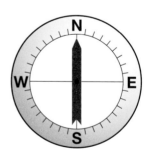

You need to know two things when you describe a turn.

• **The direction of the turn:**

clockwise   anticlockwise

- **The amount of turn:**

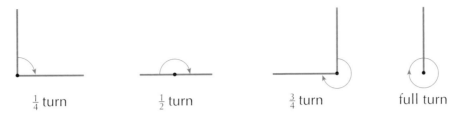

$\frac{1}{4}$ turn $\frac{1}{2}$ turn $\frac{3}{4}$ turn   full turn

Example 8.1   If you start facing South, a $\frac{1}{4}$ turn clockwise will leave you facing West.

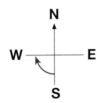

Types of angle

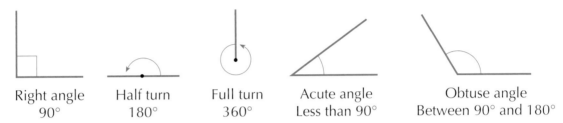

Right angle 90°   Half turn 180°   Full turn 360°   Acute angle Less than 90°   Obtuse angle Between 90° and 180°

Describing angles

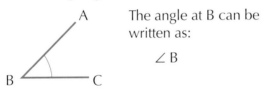

The angle at B can be written as:

$\angle B$

Describing shapes

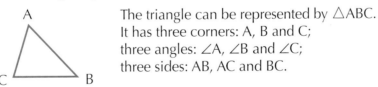

The triangle can be represented by $\triangle ABC$.
It has three corners: A, B and C;
three angles: $\angle A$, $\angle B$ and $\angle C$;
three sides: AB, AC and BC.

Example 8.2   Describe the geometric properties of these two shapes.

a   Isosceles triangle ABC

Side AB is the same length as side AC, and the angle at B is the same size as the angle at C. We write this as:

AB = AC
$\angle B = \angle C$

b   Parallelogram ABCD

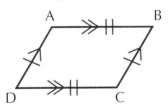

AB = CD and AD = BC
AB is parallel to CD
AD is parallel to BC

Exercise 8A

1 Describe each of the following turns in words.

a 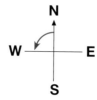   b 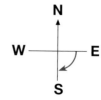   c

d 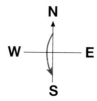   e 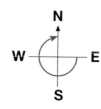   f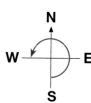

2 Copy and complete the following table.

	Starting direction	Amount of turn	Finishing direction
a	North	$\frac{1}{4}$ turn clockwise	
b	West	$\frac{1}{4}$ turn anticlockwise	
c	South	$\frac{1}{2}$ turn clockwise	
d	East	$\frac{1}{2}$ turn anticlockwise	
e	North	$\frac{3}{4}$ turn clockwise	
f	West	$\frac{3}{4}$ turn anticlockwise	

3 Write down which of the angles below are acute and which are obtuse. Estimate the size of each one in degrees.

a   b   c   d

4 For the shape ABCDE:

a Write down two lines that are equal in length.
b Write down two lines that are parallel.
c Write down two lines that are perpendicular to each other.
d Copy the diagram and draw on the two diagonals BD and CE. What do you notice about the two diagonals?

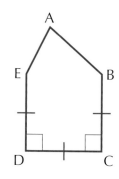

5 Write down the different properties of these three shapes.

a Equilateral triangle ABC
b Square ABCD
c Rhombus ABCD

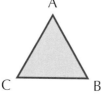   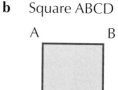

6 Write down four different places in the classroom where you can see:

   a   parallel lines   **b**   perpendicular lines

Extension Work

Word shapes

Words can be shown by writing them as the shapes they describe.
For example:

STRAIGHT LINE   O_BTUSE

Write the following as word shapes.

   PARALLEL LINES   PERPENDICULAR   RIGHT ANGLE   ACUTE
         TRIANGLES   RECTANGLES

Make up some word shapes of your own.

Calculating angles

You can calculate the **unknown angles** in a diagram by looking at the angles you do know. Unknown angles are usually written as letters, such as a, b, c, … .

Remember: some diagrams are not to scale, so you can't measure the angle using a protractor.

Angles around a point

Angles around a point add up to 360°.

Example 8.3 Calculate the size of the angle a.

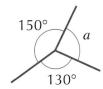

$a = 360° - 150° - 130°$
$a = 80°$

Angles on a straight line

Angles on a straight line add up to 180°.

Example 8.4 Calculate the size of the angle b.

$b = 180° - 155°$
$b = 25°$

101

Exercise 8B

1 Calculate the size of each unknown angle.

a

b

c
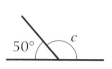

d

2 Calculate the size of each unknown angle.

a

b

c
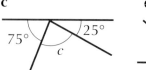

d

e
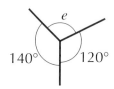

f
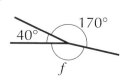

3 Calculate the size of each unknown angle.

a
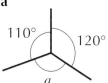

b

c
d
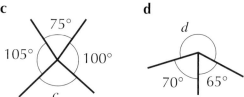

Extension **Work**

Calculate the size of each unknown angle.

1

2
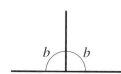

3

4

5
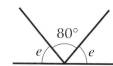

6

Coordinates

We use **coordinates** to locate a point on a grid.

The grid consists of two axes, called the **x-axis** and the **y-axis**. They are perpendicular to each other.

The two axes meet at a point called the **origin**, which is labelled O.

The point A on the grid is 4 units across and 3 units up.

We say that the coordinates of A are (4, 3), which is usually written as A(4, 3).

The first number, 4, is the **x-coordinate** of A and the second number, 3, is the **y-coordinate** of A. The x-coordinate is *always* written first.

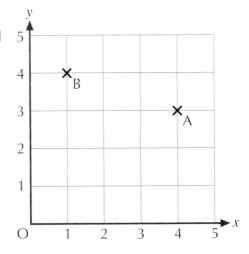

When plotting a point on a grid, a ✕ or a ● is usually used.

The coordinates of the origin are (0, 0) and the coordinates of the point B are (1, 4).

Exercise 8C

1 Write down the coordinates of the points P, Q, R, S and T.

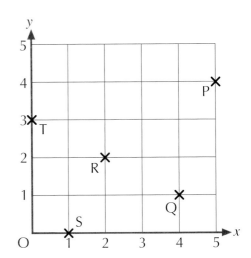

2 a Make a copy of the grid in Question 1. Then plot the points A(1, 1), B(1, 5) and C(4, 5).

b The three points are the corners of a rectangle. Plot point D to complete the rectangle.

c Write down the coordinates of D.

3 The square ABCD is drawn on the grid on the right.

a Write down the coordinates of A, B, C and D.

b The point E is halfway between points A and B. Write down the coordinates of E.

c The point F is the mid-point of the line AD. Write down the coordinates of F.

d G is the point at the centre of the square. Write down the coordinates of G.

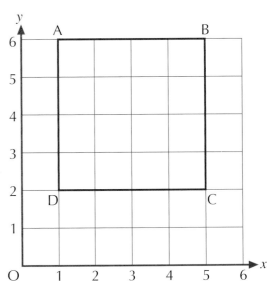

4 Various points with their letters are plotted on the grid below.

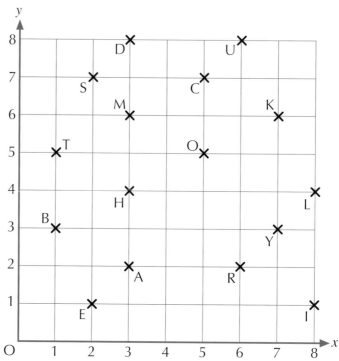

The coordinate code for the word STAR is (2, 7), (1, 5), (3, 2), (6, 2).

a Write down the coordinate code for each of these words.
  i CAKE
  ii MATHS
  iii MOBILE
  iv HOLIDAY

b Ben sends a message to Tom written in coordinate code. His message reads:
  (2, 7), (2, 1), (2, 1), (7, 3), (5, 5), (6, 8), (3, 2), (1, 5), (1, 3), (6, 2), (2, 1), (3, 2), (7, 6)
  What is Ben's message?

c Draw a different grid with points and letters. Make up your own coordinate code messages.

Extension Work

Coordinates and lines

- Draw on a grid x-and y-axes from 0 to 8.
- Plot the points (5, 0) and (5, 8) and join them to make a straight line.
- Write down the coordinates of other points that lie on the line.
- Notice that the x-coordinate of all the points is 5. We say that the equation of the line is $x = 5$.
- Now plot the points (0, 4) and (8, 4) and join them to make a straight line.
- Write down the coordinates of other points that lie on the line.
- Notice that the y-coordinate of all the points is 4. We say that the equation of the line is $y = 4$.
- Now draw lines on different grids with the following equations:
  a $x = 2$ **b** $x = 7$ **c** $x = 3\frac{1}{2}$ **d** $y = 3$ **e** $y = 6\frac{1}{2}$ **f** $y = 0$

3
I know the names for different types of angles.
I can use points of the compass.

4
I can estimate angles.
I can plot coordinates in the first quadrant.

5
I know that angles on a straight line add up to 180°.
I know that angles around a point add up to 360°
I know the properties of simple 2-D shapes.

National Test questions

1 *2006 3–5 Paper 2*

a Look at this quadrilateral.

Which **angle** is **biggest**? Tick (✓)
the correct below.

☐ Angle *a*   ☐ Angle *b*

☐ Angle *c*   ☐ Angle *d*

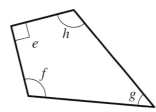

b Now look at this quadrilateral.

Angle *e* is marked with straight lines.

What does this tell you about the
angle?

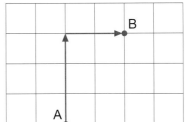

2 *2006 3–5 Paper 2*

To move from **A** to **B** on the square grid:

move **North 3**

then **East 2**

North

3

a Write the missing direction.

To move from C to D on the square grid:

    move **East 3**

    then ......

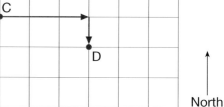

b Write the missing directions.

To move **around the four sides of a square** on the square grid:

    Move **West 1**

    then ....

    then ....

    then ....

North

3 *2001 Paper 1*

a The point K is halfway between points B and C.

What are the coordinates of point K?

b Shape ABCD is a rectangle.

What are the coordinates of point D?

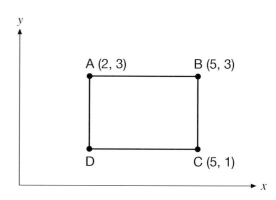

4 *2007 3–5 Paper 2*

Look at the graph.

a Write down the coordinates of points **A** and **C**.

b Point **D** can be marked so that **ABCD** is a rectangle.

Mark point D accurately on the graph.

5 *2004 3–5 Paper 2*

This diagram is not drawn accurately.

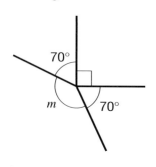

Calculate the size of *m*.

Show your working.

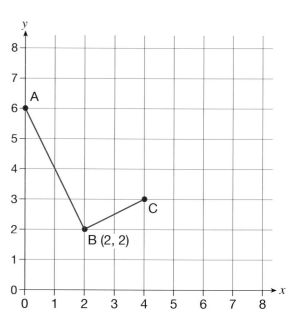

CHAPTER (9) Statistics 2

This chapter is going to show you

- How to collect and organise data
- How to create data collection forms
- How to create questionnaires
- How to use frequency tables to collate data
- How to conduct surveys and experiments

What you should already know

- How to create a tally chart
- How to draw bar charts and pictograms

Using a tally chart

What method of transport do pupils use to travel to school – and why?

When pupils are asked this question, they will give different ways of travelling, such as bus, car, bike, walking, train and even some others we don't yet know about!

A good way to collect this data is to fill in a tally chart as each pupil is asked how he or she travels to school. For example:

Type of transport	Tally	Frequency
Bus	⊦⊦⊦⊦ IIII	9
Car	⊦⊦⊦⊦	5
Bike	II	2
Walking	⊦⊦⊦⊦ ⊦⊦⊦⊦ IIII	14
Other		
	Total	30

In answering the question 'Why?', the pupils give the sorts of answers listed below.

Bus	Because it's quicker. Because it's too far to walk.
Car	My mum goes that way to work. There's no bus and it's too far. It's easier than the bus.
Bike	It's better than walking.
Walking	It's not too far. It's better than a crowded bus.

After the survey, you look at all the reasons given. Then pick out those which are given by many students. These reasons can be left as a table, or shown in other different ways.

Exercise **9A**

3

FM **1** Use your own class tally sheet (or the one on page 109) to draw a chart showing the methods of transport used by pupils to get to school, and the reasons why.

FM **2** A class were asked: 'Where would you like to go for our form trip?' They voted as follows:

Place	Tally
Alton Towers	
Camelot	ЖН I
Blackpool	ЖН III
London	III
Bath	IIII

a Draw a chart showing the places the pupils wanted to go to.

b Why do you think the pupils voted for the places given in the chart?

Extension Work

4

Put into a spreadsheet the data from one of the tally charts in this lesson.
Then create the statistical charts available.

Using the correct data

There are many different newspapers about. Can you list six different national newspapers?

Now consider Ted's question. The strict way to answer this would be to count, in each newspaper, all the words and all their letters. But this would take too long, so we take what is called a **sample**. We count, say, 100 words from each newspaper to find the length of each word.

Do certain newspapers use more long words than the other newspapers?

3

Exercise 9B

Each of these two questions is a class activity.

1 **a** You will be given either a whole newspaper or a page from one.

b Create a data collection sheet (a tally chart) like the one below.

Number of letters	Tally	Frequency
1		
2		
3		
4		
5		

c Choose a typical page from the newspaper. Then select at least two different articles. Next, count the number of letters in each word from each article (or paragraph), and fill in the tally chart. Do not miss out any words. Before you start to count, see part **f** below.

d Decide what to do with such things as:
Numbers – '6' would count as 1, 'six' would count as 3.
Hyphenated words – Ignore the hyphen.
Abbreviations – Just count what letters are there.

e Once you have completed this task, fill in the frequency column. Now create a bar chart of the results.

f Each of you will have taken a different newspaper. So what about comparing your results with others'?

2

Which newspapers have the shortest sentences?

a You will be given either a whole newspaper or a page from one.

b Make a data collection sheet (tally chart) with these headings:
Number of words   Tally   Frequency

c Choose at least two articles in the newspaper.

d Count the number of words in each sentence of each article. Fill in the tally chart as you go along.

e Check that you have used between 50 and 100 sentences. If not, choose more articles to get this number of sentences.

f Once you have used over 50 sentences, fill in the frequency column.

g Draw a bar chart from your results.

Grouped frequencies

How long does it take you to get to school in the morning?

A class was asked this question and the replies, in minutes, were:

6 min, 3 min, 5 min, 20 min, 15 min, 11 min, 13 min, 28 min, 30 min, 5 min, 2 min, 6 min, 8 min, 18 min, 23 min, 22 min, 17 min, 13 min, 4 min, 2 min, 30 min, 17 min, 19 min, 25 min, 8 min, 3 min, 9 min, 12 min, 15 min, 8 min

There are too many different values here to make a sensible bar chart. So we group them to produce a **grouped frequency table**, as shown below. The different groups which the data has been put into are called **classes**. Where possible, classes are kept the same size as each other.

Time (minutes)	0–5	6–10	11–15	16–20	21–25	26+
Frequency	7	6	6	5	3	3

A bar chart has been drawn from this data.

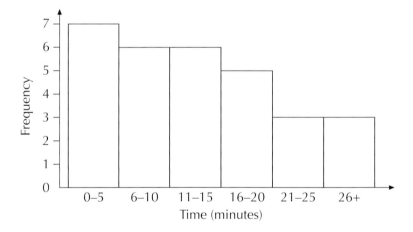

Exercise 9C

1 A class did a survey on how many pencils each pupil had with them in school. The results of this survey are:

4, 7, 2, 18, 1, 16, 19, 15, 13, 0, 9, 17, 4, 6, 10, 12, 15, 8, 3, 14, 19, 14, 15, 18, 5, 16, 3, 6, 5, 18, 12

a Put this data into a grouped frequency table with a class size of 5. That is:
0–4, 5 –9, 10–14, 15–19

b Draw a bar chart of the data.

2 A teacher asked her class: 'How many hours a week do you spend on a computer?'

She asked them to give an average, rounded figure in hours. These are their answers:

3, 6, 9, 2, 23, 18, 6, 8, 29, 27, 2, 1, 0, 5, 19, 23, 30, 21, 7, 4, 23, 8, 7, 1, 0, 25, 24, 8, 13, 18, 15, 16

a Put the above data into a grouped frequency table using these classes:

0–5, 6–10, 11–15, 16–20, 21–25, 26–30

These are some of the reasons pupils gave for the length of time they spent on a computer:

'I haven't got one.' 'I play games on mine.' 'I always try to do my homework on the computer.' 'I can't use it when I want to, because my brother's always on it.'

b Draw a bar chart from your frequency table. Try to include in the chart the reasons given.

Extension Work

A teacher asked his class: 'How many minutes do you normally spend doing your maths homework?'

Below are the pupils' answers in minutes:

60, 30, 35, 12, 30, 40, 5, 45, 25, 30, 45, 15, 40, 35, 45, 25, 60, 25, 55, 50, 35, 45, 30, 40, 16, 25, 30, 40, 15, 18, 25, 50, 35, 25, 35, 14, 40, 30, 25, 60

a Put these data into a grouped frequency table with a class size of 10. Then draw a bar chart.

b Put these data into a grouped frequency table with a class size of 30. Then draw a bar chart.

c Which class size seems more sensible to use and why?

Data collection

Let us ask a sample of the pupils in our school these questions. In other words, not everyone, but a few from each group.

You ask each question, then immediately complete your data collection sheet.

An example of a suitable data collection sheet is shown below.

Year group	Boy or girl	How much to charge?	Time to start?	Time to finish?	What would you like to eat?
Y7	B	£1	7 pm	11 pm	Crisps, beefburgers, chips
Y7	G	50p	7 pm	9 pm	Chips, crisps, lollies
Y8	G	£2	7:30 pm	10 pm	Crisps, hot dogs
Y11	B	£3	8:30 pm	11.30 pm	Chocolate, pizza

Keep track of the age	Try to ask equal numbers	Once the data are collected, they can be sorted into frequency tables.

There are five stages in running this type of survey:
- Deciding what questions to ask and who to ask.
- Making a simple, suitable data collection sheet for all the questions.
- Asking the questions and completing the data collection sheet.
- After collecting all the data, sorting them to make frequency tables.
- Analysing the data to draw conclusions from the survey.

The size of your sample will depend on many things. It may be simply the first 50 people you come across. Or you may want 10% of the available people.

In the above example, a good sample would probably be about four from each class, two boys and two girls.

Exercise 9D

A class did the above survey on a sample of 10 pupils from each of the Key Stage 3 years. Their data collection chart is shown on the next page.

1 a Create a tally chart like the one below for the suggested charges from each year group Y7, Y8 and Y9.

Charge	Tally	Frequency
25p		
50p		
75p		
£1.00		
£1.25		
£1.50		
£2.00		
£2.50		
£3.00		

b Comment on the differences between the year groups.

2 **a** Create a tally chart for the suggested finishing times from each year group Y7, Y8 and Y9.

b Comment on the differences between the year groups.

Data Collection Chart

Year group	Boy or girl	How much to charge	Time to start	Time to finish	What would you like to eat?
Y7	B	£1	7 pm	11 pm	Crisps, beefburgers, chips
Y7	G	50p	7 pm	9 pm	Chips, crisps, lollies
Y8	G	£2	7:30 pm	10 pm	Crisps, hot dogs
Y9	B	£3	8:30 pm	11:30 pm	Chocolate, pizza
Y9	G	£2	8 pm	10 pm	Pizza
Y9	B	£2.50	7:30 pm	9:30 pm	Hot dogs, Chocolate
Y8	G	£1	8 pm	10:30 pm	Crisps
Y7	B	75p	7 pm	9 pm	Crisps, beefburgers
Y7	B	£1	7:30 pm	10:30 pm	Crisps, lollies
Y8	B	£1.50	7 pm	9 pm	Crisps, chips, hot dogs
Y9	G	£2	8 pm	11 pm	Pizza, chocolate
Y9	G	£1.50	8 pm	10:30 pm	Chips, pizza
Y9	G	£2	8 pm	11 pm	Crisps, pizza
Y7	G	£1.50	7 pm	9 pm	Crisps, lollies, chocolate
Y8	B	£2	7:30 pm	9:30 pm	Crisps, lollies, chocolate
Y8	B	£1	8 pm	10 pm	Chips, hot dogs
Y9	B	£1.50	8 pm	11 pm	Pizza
Y7	B	50p	7 pm	9:30 pm	Crisps, hot dogs
Y8	G	75p	8 pm	10:30 pm	Crisps, chips
Y9	B	£2	7:30 pm	10:30 pm	Pizza
Y8	G	£1.50	7:30 pm	10 pm	Chips, hot dogs, chocolate
Y8	B	£1.25	7 pm	9:30 pm	Chips, hot dogs, lollies
Y9	G	£3	7 pm	9:30 pm	Crisps, pizza
Y9	B	£2.50	8 pm	10:30 pm	Crisps, hot dogs
Y7	G	25p	7:30 pm	10 pm	Crisps, beefburgers, lollies
Y7	G	50p	7 pm	9 pm	Crisps, pizza
Y7	G	£1	7 pm	9:30 pm	Crisps, pizza
Y8	B	£2	8 pm	10 pm	Crisps, chips, chocolate
Y8	G	£1.50	7:30 pm	9:30 pm	Chips, beefburgers
Y7	B	£1	7:30 pm	10 pm	Crisps, lollies

3 I can draw simple information charts such as pictograms.

4 I can create bar charts.
I can represent collected data in frequency diagrams and interpret them.
I can create a simple grouped frequency chart.

National Test questions

1 *2000 Paper 2*

Mrs Price sells newspapers. The table on the right shows the number of newspapers she sold on different days.

	Number of newspapers sold
Monday	70
Tuesday	42
Wednesday	80
Thursday	55

a Copy and complete the bar chart to show the number of newspapers sold on Thursday.

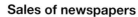

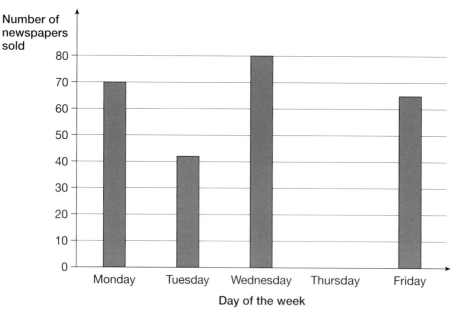

b How many newspapers did Mrs Price sell on Friday?

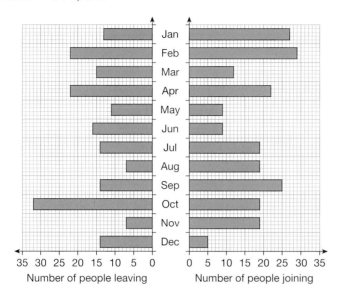

Number of people leaving   Number of people joining

Each month **some people leave** a gym and **some people join** the gym.

The diagram shows how many people leave and how many join.

a In which month did the greatest number of people **leave** the gym?

b In **September**, more people joined the gym than left the gym.

How many more?

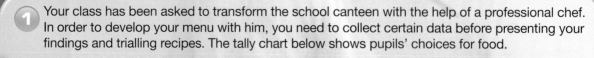

FM Be a school chef for a day

1 Your class has been asked to transform the school canteen with the help of a professional chef. In order to develop your menu with him, you need to collect certain data before presenting your findings and trialling recipes. The tally chart below shows pupils' choices for food.

	Key Stage 3	Frequency
Pasta	HHt	
Salad	II	
Pizza	HHt HHt I	
Jacket potato	HHt	
Curry	HHt HHt	
Toasties	HHt I	

	Key Stage 4	Frequency
Pasta	HHt HHt III	
Salad	IIII	
Pizza	HHt I	
Jacket potato	HHt IIII	
Curry	HHt HHt IIII	
Toasties	HHt HHt I	

a Copy and complete the frequency for each key stage.

b Draw a bar chart for each key stage.

c Use the graph to explain the differences between the two key stage choices.

2 You now have to work out how your menu will be priced with the chef. In order to do this you need to know how much pupils will be prepared to pay for lunch each day.

Price	under £1	£1–£2	over £2
Y7	30	45	12
Y8	25	50	18
Y9	18	42	25
Y10	11	52	27
Y11	8	55	22

a How many of each year group were asked in the survey?

b Draw a bar chart for each year group.

c Explain the differences between the year groups.

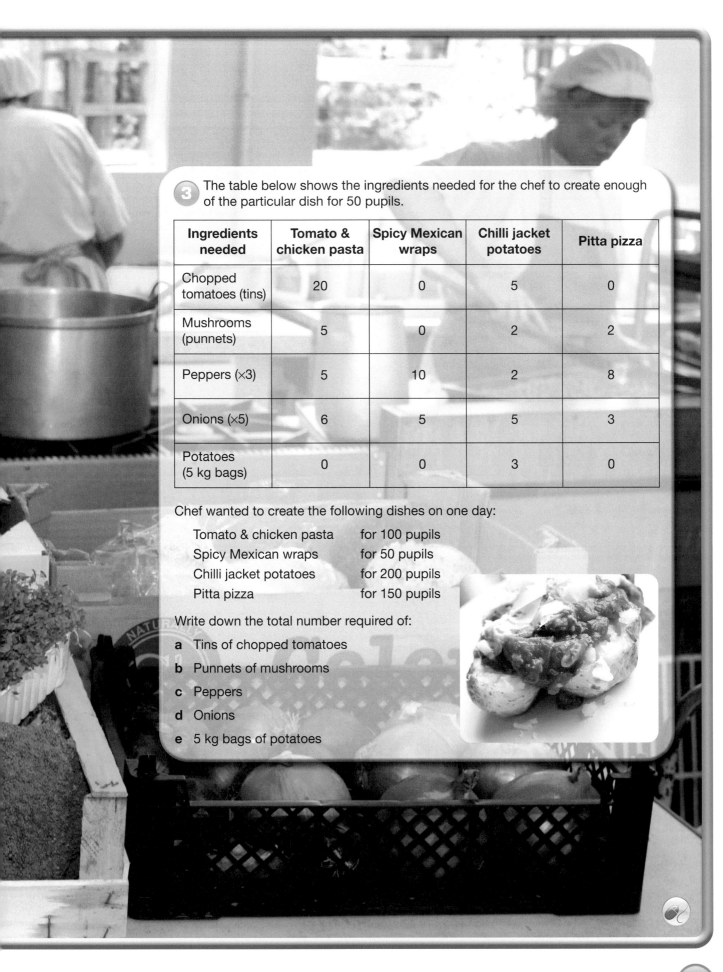

3 The table below shows the ingredients needed for the chef to create enough of the particular dish for 50 pupils.

Ingredients needed	Tomato & chicken pasta	Spicy Mexican wraps	Chilli jacket potatoes	Pitta pizza
Chopped tomatoes (tins)	20	0	5	0
Mushrooms (punnets)	5	0	2	2
Peppers (×3)	5	10	2	8
Onions (×5)	6	5	5	3
Potatoes (5 kg bags)	0	0	3	0

Chef wanted to create the following dishes on one day:

Tomato & chicken pasta   for 100 pupils
Spicy Mexican wraps   for 50 pupils
Chilli jacket potatoes   for 200 pupils
Pitta pizza   for 150 pupils

Write down the total number required of:

a Tins of chopped tomatoes

b Punnets of mushrooms

c Peppers

d Onions

e 5 kg bags of potatoes

This chapter is going to show you

- How to round off positive whole numbers
- The order of operations
- How to multiply and divide a three-digit whole number by a single-digit whole number without a calculator
- How to use a calculator efficiently

What you should already know

- Two, five and ten times tables
- Place value of the digits in a number such as 23.508

Rounding

What is wrong with this picture?

It shows that the woman's weight (60 kg) balances the man's weight (110 kg) when both weights are rounded to the nearest 100 kg!

This example highlights the need to round numbers *sensibly*, depending on the situation in which they occur.

But, we do not always need numbers to be precise, and it is easier to work with numbers that are rounded off.

Example 10.1 ▷ Round off each of these numbers to: **i** the nearest 10 **ii** the nearest 100 **iii** the nearest 1000.

a 937 **b** 2363 **c** 3799 **d** 285

a 937 is 940 to the nearest 10, 900 to the nearest 100 and 1000 to the nearest 1000.

b 2363 is 2360 to the nearest 10, 2400 to the nearest 100, and 2000 to the nearest 1000.

c 3799 is 3800 to the nearest 10, 3800 to the nearest 100, and 4000 to the nearest 1000.

d 285 is 290 to nearest 10 (halfway values round up), 300 to the nearest 100, and 0 to the nearest 1000.

Example 10.2 ▷ Round off each of these numbers to the nearest whole number.

a 9.35 **b** 5.99

a 9.35 is 9 to the nearest whole number.

b 5.99 is 6 to the nearest whole number.

Exercise 10A

1 Round off each of these numbers to: **i** the nearest 10 **ii** the nearest 100 **iii** the nearest 1000.

a 3731 **b** 807 **c** 2111 **d** 4086 **e** 265 **f** 3457
g 4050 **h** 2999 **i** 1039 **j** 192 **k** 3192 **l** 964

2 **i** What is the mass being weighed by each scale to the nearest 100 g?

ii Estimate the mass being weighed to the nearest 10 g.

a  **b**  **c**  **d**

3 **i** What is the volume of the liquid in each measuring cylinder to the nearest 10 ml?

ii Estimate the volume of liquid to the nearest whole number.

a 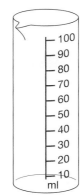 **b** 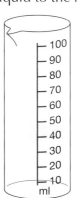 **c** 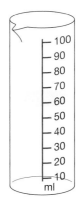 **d**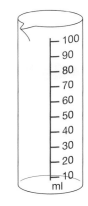

4 Round off each of these numbers to the nearest whole number.

a 4.72 **b** 3.07 **c** 2.634 **d** 1.932 **e** 0.78 **f** 0.92
g 3.92 **h** 2.64 **i** 3.18 **j** 3.475 **k** 1.45 **l** 1.863

5 How long is each of these ropes to: **i** the nearest 10 cm? **ii** the nearest cm?

a **b**

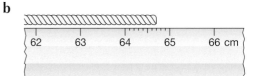

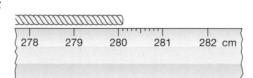

c

278 279 280 281 282 cm

d

3.4 3.5 3.6 3.7 3.8 m

6 The following are the diameters of the planets in kilometres. Round off each one to the nearest 1000 km. Then place the planets in order of size, starting with the smallest.

Planet	Earth	Jupiter	Mars	Mercury	Neptune	Pluto	Saturn	Uranus	Venus
Diameter (km)	12 800	142 800	6780	5120	49 500	2284	120 660	51 100	12 100

Extension **Work**

Rounding to one decimal place

Most of the time, we do not need to be too accurate. Usually an accuracy of one decimal place (1 dp) is enough. For example:

9.37 is 9.4 to 1 dp   4.323 is 4.3 to 1 dp   5.99 is 6.0 to 1 dp

Round off to 1 dp the numbers in Exercise 10A, Question 4.

The four operations

Example 10.3

a Find the product of 9 and 6.

b Find the remainder when 347 is divided by 5.

a Product means 'multiply'. So, $9 \times 6 = 54$.

b Using short division gives:

$$\begin{array}{r} 6\,9 \\ \overline{5)3\,4\,{}^{4}7} \end{array}$$

The remainder is $47 - 45 = 2$.

Example 10.4

a Find the difference between 453 and 237.

b Work out 43×4.

a Set out the problem in columns:

$$\begin{array}{r} {}^{4}\cancel{5}{}^{1}3 \\ -\,2\,3\,7 \\ \hline 2\,1\,6 \end{array}$$

You have to borrow from the tens column because 7 cannot be taken from 3.

b Using grid multiplication gives:

×	40	3
4	160	12

So, $43 \times 4 = 160 + 12 = 172$.

Example 10.5

How long does a train journey take when the train leaves at 10:32 am and arrives at 1:12 pm?

Draw a blank number line in hours, as shown. Then count on along the line.

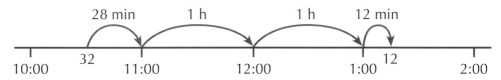

The answer is:

1h + 1h + 28 min + 12 min = 2h 40 min.

Exercise 10B

1 Write down the answer to each of these.

a $3 \times 6 = \ldots$	**b** $6 \times 3 = \ldots$	**c** $6 \times 7 = \ldots$	**d** $4 \times 2 = \ldots$
e $5 \times 5 = \ldots$	**f** $2 \times 8 = \ldots$	**g** $4 \times 5 = \ldots$	**h** $8 \times 0 = \ldots$
i $6 \times 10 = \ldots$	**j** $7 \times 1 = \ldots$	**k** $4 \times 7 = \ldots$	**l** $10 \times 10 = \ldots$
m $9 \times 8 = \ldots$	**n** $9 \times 6 = \ldots$	**o** $9 \times 3 = \ldots$	**p** $5 \times 9 = \ldots$
q $7 \times 5 = \ldots$	**r** $7 \times 9 = \ldots$	**s** $6 \times 8 = \ldots$	**t** $7 \times 8 = \ldots$

2 Work out each of these.

a $6 \times 40 = \ldots$	**b** $5 \times 60 = \ldots$	**c** $5 \times 40 = \ldots$	**d** $60 \times 5 = \ldots$
e $70 \times 6 = \ldots$	**f** $800 \times 3 = \ldots$	**g** $6 \times 300 = \ldots$	**h** $7 \times 800 = \ldots$
i $30 \times 9 = \ldots$	**j** $50 \times 40 = \ldots$		

3 Copy each of these grids and fill in the gaps.

a 34×7 $\begin{array}{c|cc} \times & 30 & 4 \\ \hline 7 & & \end{array}$
b 26×4 $\begin{array}{c|cc} \times & 20 & 6 \\ \hline 4 & & \end{array}$
c 52×7 $\begin{array}{c|cc} \times & 50 & 2 \\ \hline 7 & & \end{array}$

4 Use the grid method as in Question 3, or any other method, to find:

a 58×7	**b** 35×8	**c** 34×2	**d** 19×8
e 32×6	**f** 42×7	**g** 56×6	**h** 33×3

5 Find the sum and product of: **a** 7 and 20   **b** 2 and 50

 6 The local video shop is having a sale. Videos are £4.99 each or five for £20.

   a What is the cost of three videos?

   b What is the cost of ten videos?

   c What is the greatest number of video you can buy with £37?

7 a Three consecutive integers have a sum of 90. What are they?

   b Two consecutive integers have a product of 132. What are they?

   c Explain why there is more than one answer to this problem:
       Two consecutive integers have a difference of 1. What are they?

Extension **Work**

The magic number of this magic square is 50.

That means that the numbers in every row, in every column and in both diagonals add up to 50.

However, there are many more ways to make 50 by adding four numbers. For example, each of the following sets of 4 numbers makes 50.

5	18	11	16
12	15	6	17
14	9	20	7
19	8	13	10

5	18
12	15

5	16
19	10

18	11
8	13

How many more arrangements of four numbers can you find that add up to 50?

BODMAS

The following are instructions for making a cup of tea.

Can you put them in the right order?

Drink tea	Empty teapot	Fill kettle	Put milk in cup	Put teabag in teapot
Switch on kettle	Wait for tea to brew	Rinse teapot with hot water	Pour boiling water in teapot	Pour out tea

It is important that things are done in the right order. There are rules about this when doing mathematical operations.

The order of operations is called **BODMAS**, which stands for **B** (Brackets), **O** (Order or POwer), **D M** (Division and Multiplication) and **A S** (Addition and Subtraction).

Operations are always done in this order, which means that brackets are done first, followed by powers, then multiplication and division, and finally addition and subtraction.

Example 10.6 Circle the operation that you do first in each of these calculations. Then work out each one.

a $2 + 6 \div 2$ **b** $32 - 4 \times 5$ **c** $6 \div 3 - 1$ **d** $6 \div (3 - 1)$

a Division is done before addition, so you get $2 + 6 \div 2 = 2 + 3 = 5$.

b Multiplication is done before subtraction, so you get $32 - 4 \times 5 = 32 - 20 = 12$.

c Division is done before subtraction, so you get $6 \div 3 - 1 = 2 - 1 = 1$.

d Brackets are done first, so you get $6 \div (3 - 1) = 6 \div 2 = 3$.

Example 10.7   Put brackets into each of these to make the calculation true.

     a $5 + 1 \times 4 = 24$ **b** $24 \div 6 - 2 = 6$

Decide which operation is done first.

     a $(5 + 1) \times 4 = 6 \times 4 = 24$

     b $24 \div (6 - 2) = 24 \div 4 = 6$

Exercise 10C

1   Copy each calculation and circle the operation that you do first. Then work out each one.

     a $2 + 3 \times 6$ **b** $12 - 6 \div 3$ **c** $5 \times 5 + 2$ **d** $12 \div 4 - 2$

     e $(2 + 3) \times 6$ **f** $(12 - 3) \div 3$ **g** $5 \times (5 + 2)$ **h** $12 \div (4 - 2)$

2   Work out each of these, showing each step of the calculation.

     a $2 \times 3 + 4$ **b** $2 \times (3 + 4)$ **c** $2 + 3 \times 4$ **d** $(2 + 3) \times 4$

     e $4 \times 4 - 4$ **f** $(2 + 3) \times (4 + 5)$ **g** $4 \div 4 + 4 \div 4$ **h** $44 \div 4 + 4$

3   Put brackets into each of the following to make the calculation true.

     a $2 \times 5 + 4 = 18$ **b** $2 + 6 \times 3 = 24$ **c** $2 + 3 \times 1 + 6 = 35$

     d $3 \times 4 + 3 + 7 = 28$ **e** $3 + 4 \times 7 + 1 = 35$ **f** $3 + 4 \times 7 + 1 = 50$

     g $9 - 5 - 2 = 6$ **h** $9 - 5 \times 2 = 8$ **i** $4 + 4 + 4 \div 2 = 6$

4   Work out the value of each of these.

     a $(4 + 4) \div (4 + 4)$ **b** $(4 \times 4) \div (4 + 4)$ **c** $(4 + 4 + 4) \div 4$

     d $4 \times (4 - 4) + 4$ **e** $(4 \times 4 + 4) \div 4$ **f** $(4 + 4 + 4) \div 2$

     g $4 + 4 - 4 \div 4$ **h** $(4 + 4) \times (4 \div 4)$ **i** $(4 + 4) + 4 \div 4$

5   Work out the value of each expression in your head.

     a $2 + (4 \times 10) = \dots\dots$ **b** $(2 \times 5) + 10 = \dots\dots$ **c** $5 + (20 \div 5) = \dots\dots$

     d $(2 + 4) \times 10 = \dots\dots$ **e** $(6 \times 4) - 3 = \dots\dots$ **f** $(5 + 20) \div 5 = \dots\dots$

     g $2 \times (5 + 10) = \dots\dots$ **h** $6 \times (4 - 3) = \dots\dots$ **i** $(100 \div 20) \times 3 = \dots\dots$

     j $100 \div (20 + 5) = \dots\dots$ **k** $(100 \div 20) + 5 = \dots\dots$ **l** $4 \times (5 - 2) = \dots\dots$

Extension Work

In Question 4, each calculation is made up of four 4s.

Work out the value of: **a** $44 \div 4 - 4$ **b** $4 \times 4 - 4 \div 4$ **c** $4 \times 4 + 4 - 4$

Can you make other calculations using four 4s to give answers that you have not yet obtained in Question 4 or in the three calculations above?

Do as many as you can and see whether you can make all the values up to 20.

Repeat with five 5s. For example:

     $(5 + 5) \div 5 - 5 \div 5 = 1$ $(5 \times 5 - 5) \div (5 + 5) = 2$

Multiplication and division

Example 10.8 Work out 36 × 4.

Below are three examples of the ways this calculation can be done. The answer is 144.

Box method (partitioning)

×	30	6	
4	120	24	144

Column method (expanded working)

$$
\begin{array}{r}
36 \\
\times\ \ 4 \\
\hline
24 \quad (4 \times 6) \\
120 \quad (4 \times 30) \\
\hline
144
\end{array}
$$

Column method (compacted working)

$$
\begin{array}{r}
36 \\
\times\ \ 4 \\
\hline
144 \\
{\scriptstyle 2}
\end{array}
$$

Example 10.9 Work out 543 ÷ 8.

Below are two examples of the ways this can be done. The answer is 67, remainder 7.

Subtracting multiples

$$
\begin{array}{r}
543 \\
-\ 320 \quad (40 \times 8) \\
\hline
223 \\
-\ 160 \quad (20 \times 8) \\
\hline
63 \\
-\ \ 48 \quad (6 \times 8) \\
\hline
15 \\
-\ 8 \quad (1 \times 8) \\
\hline
7
\end{array}
$$

Short division

$$
8\overline{)5\overset{6}{4}3}\quad 67 \text{ rem } 7
$$

Exercise 10D

1 Work out each of the following multiplication problems. Use any method you are happy with.

    a 17 × 3   **b** 32 × 4   **c** 19 × 5   **d** 56 × 6

    e 2 × 346   **f** 3 × 541   **g** 7 × 147   **h** 9 × 213

 2 A van does 34 miles to a gallon of petrol. How many miles can it do if the petrol tank holds 8 gallons?

 3 The school photocopier can print 82 sheets a minute. If it runs without stopping for 7 minutes, how many sheets will it print?

 4 Each day 7 Jumbo jets fly from London to San Francisco. Each jet can carry up to 348 passengers. How many people can travel from London to San Francisco each day?

 5 Blank CDs cost 45p each. How much will 5 CDs cost? Give your answer in pounds.

 6 A daily newspaper sells advertising by the square inch. On Monday, it sells 163 square inches at £9 per square inch. How much money does it get from this advertising?

7 Work out each division by taking away chunks (subtracting multiples). Show all your working out.

    a 79 ÷ 7   **b** 55 ÷ 3   **c** 124 ÷ 5

    d 112 ÷ 6   **e** 71 ÷ 4

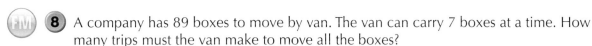
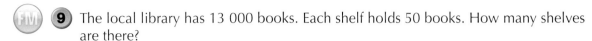

FM **8** A company has 89 boxes to move by van. The van can carry 7 boxes at a time. How many trips must the van make to move all the boxes?

FM **9** The local library has 13 000 books. Each shelf holds 50 books. How many shelves are there?

FM **10** How many bubble packs of 40 nails can be filled from a carton of 450 nails?

FM **11** **a** To raise money, Wath Running Club are going to do a relay race from Wath to Hull, which is 84 kilometres. Each runner will run 8 kilometres. How many runners will be needed to cover the distance?

b Sponsorship will bring in £9 per kilometre. How much money will the club raise?

Extension **Work**

A way of multiplying two two-digit numbers together is the 'Funny Face' method.

This shows how to do 26×57.

$$26 \times 57 = (20 + 6) \times (50 + 7)$$

$$(20 + 6) \times (50 + 7) \qquad \begin{array}{rl} 1000 & (20 \times 50) \\ 140 & (20 \times 7) \\ 300 & (6 \times 50) \\ + \ \ 42 & (6 \times 7) \\ \hline 1482 & \end{array}$$

Do a poster showing a calculation using the 'Funny Face' method.

Efficient calculations

A quick way to check whether an answer is right is to estimate the answer.

Example 10.10 Work out: **a** 30×400 **b** $3000 \div 15$

a $30 \times 400 = 3 \times 10 \times 4 \times 100 = 12\,000$

b $3000 \div 15 = \dfrac{3000}{15} = \dfrac{\overset{2}{\cancel{3000}}}{\cancel{15}} = 200$

Example 10.11 Estimate the answer to each of these: **a** 31×53 **b** $3127 \div 60$

a $31 \times 53 \approx 30 \times 50 = 1500$ (Correct answer is 1643.)

b $\dfrac{3127}{60} \approx \dfrac{3000}{60} = \dfrac{\overset{5}{\cancel{3000}}}{\cancel{60}} = 50$ (Correct answer is 52.1 to 1 dp.)

Exercise 10E **1** Work out the following.

a 2×10	**b** 20×10	**c** 7×10	**d** 70×20	**e** 30×40	**f** 30×70
g 20×40	**h** 50×60	**i** 70×20	**j** 60×30	**k** 40×80	**l** 30×30
m 60×70	**n** 20×20	**o** 80×30	**p** 50×50	**q** 60×40	**r** 70×70

2 Three answers are given for each calculation. Which one is correct?

a 20×90 180, 1800, 18 000   **b** 300×40 120, 1200, 12 000

c 50×400 2000, 20 000, 200 000   **d** 7×60 420, 4200, 42 000

3 Work out the following.

a $1200 \div 40$	**b** $200 \div 40$	**c** $1400 \div 20$	**d** $1400 \div 70$
e $1500 \div 50$	**f** $1600 \div 100$	**g** $1800 \div 30$	**h** $4000 \div 40$
i $2000 \div 40$	**j** $2400 \div 60$	**k** $1800 \div 60$	**l** $1500 \div 30$
m $4000 \div 20$	**n** $2800 \div 40$	**o** $3500 \div 70$	

4 Estimate the answer for each of these.

a 23×11 **b** 43×12 **c** 72×18 **d** 32×42 **e** 31×69

f 18×38 **g** 48×58 **h** 72×22 **i** 63×33 **j** 39×81

5 Estimate the answer for each of these.

a $1178 \div 32$ **b** $207 \div 38$ **c** $1412 \div 22$ **d** $1378 \div 68$ **e** $1534 \div 48$

f $1578 \div 98$ **g** $1824 \div 32$ **h** $1998 \div 37$ **i** $1998 \div 41$ **j** $2376 \div 62$

6 Estimate the answer for each of these.

a $\dfrac{194 + 816}{122 + 90}$ **b** $\dfrac{213 + 73}{63 - 13}$ **c** $\dfrac{132 + 88}{78 - 28}$ **d** $\dfrac{792 + 88}{54 - 21}$

7 **a** On squared paper, draw a shape that is ten times bigger in both directions than the shape on the right.

How many little squares are there in the larger shape?

b Repeat part **a** with the shape on the right.

c Without drawing, work out how many squares there would be in a shape that is 100 times bigger than the shape in part **a**.

Extension **Work**

Multiplications and divisions which have lots of zeros can cause difficulties if done using a calculator.

Use mental methods to work out the following.

The first two questions are done for you.

1 Use mental methods to work out $30\,000 \times 4\,000\,000$.

$$30\,000 \times 4\,000\,000 = 3 \times 4 \times 10\,000 \times 1\,000\,000$$
$$= 12 \times 10\,000\,000\,000$$
$$= 120\,000\,000\,000$$

2 Estimate the value of $\dfrac{8\,125\,751}{412\,075}$.

$$\frac{8\,125\,751}{412\,075} \approx \frac{8\,000\,000}{400\,000} = \frac{8\,0\!\!\!/0\!\!\!/0\,0\!\!\!/0\!\!\!/0\!\!\!/}{4\,0\!\!\!/0\!\!\!/0\,0\!\!\!/0\!\!\!/0\!\!\!/} = 20$$

3 Use mental methods to work out $7\,000\,000\,000 \times 6\,000\,000$.

4 Use mental methods to estimate the value of $7\,129\,836 \times 29\,451$.

5 Estimate the value of $\dfrac{2\,017\,832}{510\,965}$.

Calculating with measurements

Below are the common metric units which you need to know. Also given are the relationships between these units.

Length

1 kilometre (km) = 1000 metres (m)
1 metre (m) = 100 centimetres (cm)
1 centimetre (cm) = 10 millimetres (mm)

Capacity

1 litre (l) = 100 centilitres (l)
1 litre (l) = 1000 millilitres (ml)

Mass

1 kilogram (kg) = 1000 grams (g)

Example 10.12 A recipe needs 550 grams of flour to make a cake. How many 1 kg bags of flour will be needed to make six cakes?

Six cakes will need 6 × 550 = 3300 g, which will need four bags of flour.

Example 10.13 What unit would you use to measure each of these?

a Width of a football field

b Length of a pencil

c Weight of a car

d Spoonful of medicine

Choose a sensible unit. Sometimes there is more than one answer.

a Metre   **b** Centimetre   **c** Kilogram   **d** Millilitre

Example 10.14 Convert: **a** 6 cm to mm   **b** 1250 g to kg   **c** 5 l to cl

You need to know the conversion factors.

a 1 cm = 10 mm: 6 × 10 = 60 mm

b 1000 g = 1 kg: 1250 ÷ 1000 = 1.25 kg

c 1 l = 100 cl: 5 l = 5 × 100 = 500 cl

Exercise 10F

1 Convert each of the following lengths to centimetres.

    a 60 mm   **b** 2 m   **c** 743 mm   **d** 0.007 km   **e** 12.35 m

2 Convert each of the following lengths to kilometres.

    a 456 m   **b** 7645 m   **c** 6532 cm   **d** 21 358 mm   **e** 54 m

3 Convert each of the following lengths to millimetres.

    a 34 cm   **b** 3 m   **c** 3 km   **d** 35.6 cm   **e** 0.7 cm

4 Convert each of the following masses to kilograms.

    a 3459 g   **b** 215 g   **c** 65 120 g   **d** 21 g   **e** 210 g

5 Convert each of the following masses to grams.

    a 4 kg   **b** 4.32 kg   **c** 0.56 kg   **d** 0.007 kg   **e** 6.784 kg

6 Convert each of the following capacities to litres.

    a 237 cl   **b** 3097 ml   **c** 1862 cl   **d** 48 cl   **e** 96 427 ml

7 Convert each of the following times to hours and minutes.

    a 70 min   **b** 125 min   **c** 87 min   **d** 200 min   **e** 90 min

(FM) **8** Fill in each missing unit.

    a A two-storey house is about 7…… high   **b** John weighs about 47……

    c Mary lives about 2…… from school   **d** Ravid ran a marathon in 3……

9 Read the value from each of the following scales. Write down each value.

    a   **b**   **c**

    d   **e**   **f**

Extension Work

Area is measured in square millimetres (mm²), square centimetres (cm²), square metres (m²) and square kilometres (km²).

This square shows 1 square centimetre reproduced exactly.

You can fit 100 square millimetres inside this square because a 1 centimetre square is 10 mm by 10 mm.

So 1 cm² = 100 mm².

1 What unit would you use to measure the area of each of these?

    a Football field   **b** Photograph   **c** Fingernail

    d National park   **e** Pacific Ocean   **f** Stamp

2 Convert: **a** 24 cm² to mm²

              b 4000 mm² to cm²

3 Look up the areas of some countries on the Internet or in an encyclopaedia.

    a Which are the three biggest countries (in terms of area) in the world?

    b Which is the biggest country (in terms of area) in Europe?

Solving problems

Mrs Farmer is frightened of mice. One day, she finds three mice in her kitchen.
A large one, a medium-sized one and a small one.

She tries to scare them out, but they are Mathematical Mice who will only leave when a dice is rolled.

> When the dice shows 1 or 2, the small mouse goes through the door.

> When the dice shows 3 or 4, the medium-sized mouse goes through the door.

> When the dice shows 5 or 6, the big mouse goes through the door.

For example: Mrs Farmer rolls the dice. She gets 3, so the medium-sized mouse goes through the door. Next, she rolls 5, so the big mouse goes through the door. Next, she rolls 4, so the medium-sized mouse comes back through the door. Then she rolls 2, so the small mouse leaves. Finally, she rolls 4, so the medium-sized mouse leaves and all three are out of the kitchen.

Can you find a rule for the number of throws that it takes to get all the mice out?

What if there were two mice, or six mice?

Before you start, you should think about how you are going to record your results.

You should make sure that you explain in writing what you are going to do.

If you come up with an idea, you should write it down and explain it or test it.

LEVEL BOOSTER

3
I can remember addition and subtraction facts when solving problems involving large numbers.

I can remember simple multiplication and division facts.

I can solve whole number problems involving multiplications and division, including answers with remainders.

4
I can read numbers on a range of measuring instruments.

I can round whole numbers to the nearest 10, 100 or 1000.

I know the names and abbreviations of units in everyday use.

5
I can convert between metric units.

I can multiply and divide whole numbers and decimals.

I can round numbers to one decimal place.

I can use brackets appropriately.

I can estimate answers to questions.

3

1 *2007 3–5 Paper 1*

Here are the rules for a number grid:

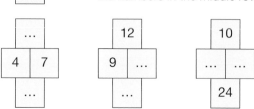

This number is the **sum** of the numbers in the middle row.

This number is the **product** of the numbers in the middle row.

Use the rules to write the missing numbers in these number grids.

FM 2 *2007 3–5 Paper 2*

Here are the costs of tickets for a concert:

a **Two adults** go to the concert with **three children**.

Altogether, how much do their tickets cost?

Concert tickets	
Adults:	£24.50 each
Children:	£16.45 each

b **Three adults** go to the concert with some children. Altogether, their tickets cost **£155.75**.

How many children went to the concert with the three adults?

FM 3 *2006 Paper 1*

A shop sells three different sized bottles of lemonade:

a I want **3 litres** of lemonade. I could buy **three** bottles of size **1 litre**.

How much would that cost?

b Write a **different way** I could buy exactly 3 litres of lemonade.

Now work out how much it would cost.

c Write another **different way** I could buy exactly 3 litres of lemonade.

Now work out how much it would cost.

d My friend buys seven bottles of lemonade. **Two** of the bottles are of size **1½** litres. **Five** of the bottles are of size **2 litres**.

How many litres is that altogether?

1 litre
39p

1½ litre
55p

2 litre
70p

4 *2006 4–6 Paper 1*

Work out the missing numbers. In each part, you can use the first line to help you.

a $16 \times 15 = 240$

$16 \times \boxed{} = 480$

b $46 \times 44 = 2024$

$46 \times 22 = \boxed{}$

c $600 \div 24 = 25$

$600 \div \boxed{} = 50$

5 *2006 4–6 Paper 2*

Write down the numbers missing from the boxes.

$4 \times \boxed{} + 20 = 180$ $\qquad$ $4 \times 20 + \boxed{} = 180$ $\qquad$ $4 \times \boxed{} - 20 = 180$

6 *2001 Paper 1*

a Write the answers to $(4 + 2) \times 3 = \ldots\ldots$, $4 + (2 \times 3) = \ldots\ldots$

b Work out the answer to $(2 + 4) \times (6 + 3 + 1) = \ldots\ldots$

c Copy and put brackets in the calculation to make the answer 50.

$4 + 5 + 1 \times 5 = 50$

d Now copy and put brackets in the calculation to make the answer 34.

$4 + 5 + 1 \times 5 = 34$

What's your carbon footprint?

Every day we use energy. Scientists can work out our carbon footprint by calculating how much energy we use each year.

Fascinating facts

Our homes use 30% of the total energy used in the UK.

- The average yearly carbon dioxide emissions in the UK are 9.4 tonnes per person.

- A rule for working out the average yearly carbon dioxide emissions of people in the USA is to multiply the UK figure by 3 and subtract 8.4. This gives $9.4 \times 3 - 8.4 = 19.8$ tonnes per person.

- If we turn down the thermostat by one degree we would save 300 kg of carbon dioxide per household per year.

- A family car with a petrol engine uses about 160 grams per kilometre, compared with about 100 grams per kilometre for a small car or 300 grams per kilometre for a large 4 × 4.

Carbon calculator

1 If you take the bus to school you can work out the emissions from a bus.
   Carbon dioxide emission (kg) = Distance (km) × 0.17

a Work out the carbon dioxide emission for a distance of 10 kilometres. Give your answer in grams.

b A school bus holds 75 passengers. Work out the carbon dioxide emissions per person.

c Work out the carbon dioxide emissions for a person travelling 10 kilometres by family car.

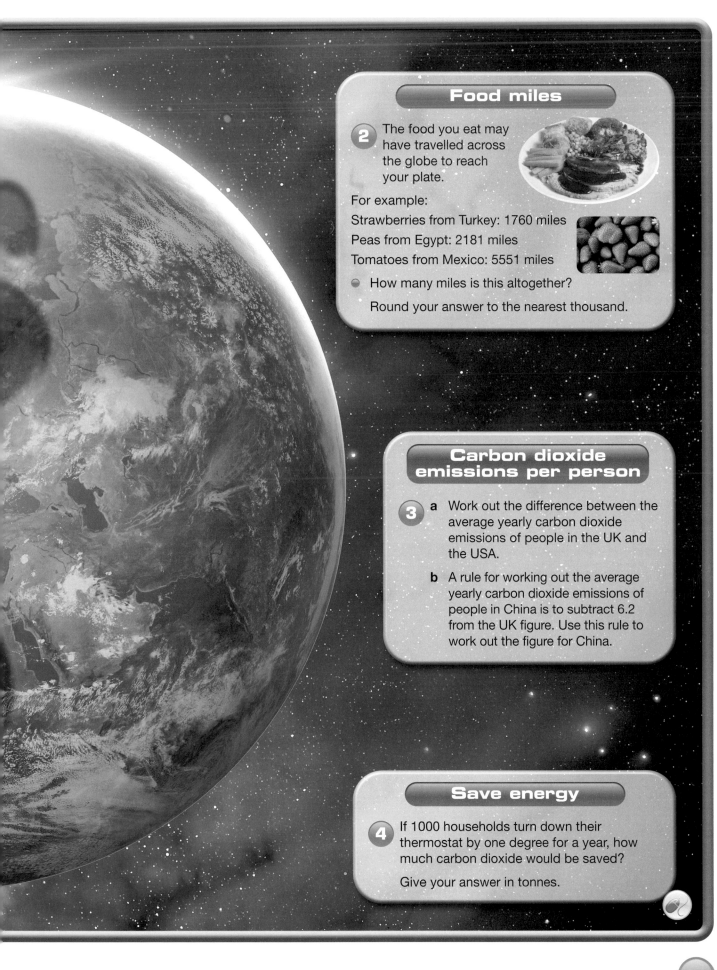

Food miles

2 The food you eat may have travelled across the globe to reach your plate.

For example:

Strawberries from Turkey: 1760 miles

Peas from Egypt: 2181 miles

Tomatoes from Mexico: 5551 miles

- How many miles is this altogether?

  Round your answer to the nearest thousand.

Carbon dioxide emissions per person

3 **a** Work out the difference between the average yearly carbon dioxide emissions of people in the UK and the USA.

b A rule for working out the average yearly carbon dioxide emissions of people in China is to subtract 6.2 from the UK figure. Use this rule to work out the figure for China.

Save energy

4 If 1000 households turn down their thermostat by one degree for a year, how much carbon dioxide would be saved?

Give your answer in tonnes.

This chapter is going to show you	What you should already know
● What square numbers and triangle numbers are ● How to draw graphs from functions	● How to find the term-to-term rule in a sequence ● How to plot coordinates

Square numbers

When we multiply any number by itself, the answer is called the **square of the number** or the **number squared**. We call this operation **squaring**. We show it by putting a small 2 at the top right-hand corner of the number being squared. For example:

$4 \times 4 = 4^2 = 16$

The result of squaring a number is called a **square number**. The first ten square numbers are shown below.

1×1	2×2	3×3	4×4	5×5	6×6	7×7	8×8	9×9	10×10
1^2	2^2	3^2	4^2	5^2	6^2	7^2	8^2	9^2	10^2
1	4	9	16	25	36	49	64	81	100

You need to learn all of these.

Exercise 11A

1 This is a table of numbers and their squares. Fill in the gaps.

Number		Number squared
3	3×3	9
5	5×5	25
	2×2	
		36
7		
	12×12	
		121
		0
		1
		81
4		

2 Look at the pattern on the right.

Pattern 1

Pattern 2

Pattern 3

a Copy this pattern and draw the next two shapes in the pattern.

b What is special about the total number of dots in each pattern number?

Pattern 1	Pattern 2	Pattern 3
1	$1 + 3$	$4 + 5$
	4	9

c What is special about the number of blue dots in each pattern number?

d What is special about the number of red dots in each pattern number?

e Write down a connection between square numbers and odd numbers.

3 Write each number below as the sum of two square numbers. Use the list of square numbers on page 109 and your answers to Question 1 to help you. The first four have been done for you.

a	$2 = 1 + 1$	**b**	$5 = 1 + 4$	**c**	$8 = 4 + 4$	**d**	$10 = 1 + 9$
e	$13 = \ +$	**f**	$17 = \ +$	**g**	$25 = \ +$	**h**	$34 = \ +$
i	$41 = \ +$	**j**	$50 = \ +$	**k**	$58 = \ +$	**l**	$65 = \ +$
m	$68 = \ +$	**n**	$73 = \ +$	**o**	$80 = \ +$	**p**	$90 = \ +$
q	$97 = \ +$	**r**	$106 = \ +$	**s**	$130 = \ +$	**t**	$162 = \ +$

Extension Work

You may have noticed from Question 3g above that $3^2 + 4^2 = 5^2$ (because $9 + 16 = 25$).

This is a *special square sum* (made up of only square numbers). There are many to be found. See which of the following pairs of squares will give you a special square sum.

$5^2 + 12^2$ $3^2 + 7^2$ $6^2 + 8^2$ $9^2 + 16^2$

$5^2 + 9^2$ $10^2 + 24^2$ $7^2 + 24^2$

Triangle numbers

Look at the triangles on the right. The number below each triangle is the number of dots inside it. These numbers form a sequence called the **triangle numbers**.

1

3

6

The first few triangle numbers are

1, 3, 6, 10, 15, 21, 28, 36, 45, ...

Exercise 11B

1 Look at the following sequence.

Pattern number	1	2	3	4	5	6	7
Number of blue dots	1	3	6				
Number of yellow dots	0	1	3				
Total number of dots	1	4	9				

a Continue the sequence for the next four shapes.

b Complete the table to show the number of dots in each shape.

c What is special about the number of **blue** dots?

d What is special about the number of **yellow** dots?

e What is special about the **total number** of dots in each pattern number?

f Write down a connection between triangle numbers and square numbers.

2 Look at the numbers in the box on the right.

Write down the numbers that are:

a square numbers. **d** multiples of 5.

b triangle numbers. **e** odd numbers.

c even numbers. **f** multiples of 3.

1	2	3	5	6	9
10	13	15	18	21	
25	26	28	29	36	
38	64	75	93	100	

3 Write each number below as the sum of two triangle numbers. Use the list of triangle numbers on page 137. The first three have been done for you.

a $4 = 1 + 3$ **b** $6 = 3 + 3$ **c** $9 = 3 + 6$ **d** $12 = \ +$

e $16 = \ +$ **f** $21 = \ +$ **g** $25 = \ +$ **h** $31 = \ +$

i $36 = \ +$ **j** $60 = \ +$ **k** $64 = \ +$ **l** $81 = \ +$

Extension Work

1 Write down the first 12 triangular numbers.

2 How many of these numbers are: **i** even? **ii** odd?

3 How many of these numbers are multiples of 3?

4 Look at the numbers that are not multiples of 3. What is special about them all?

5 Test parts **b** to **d** using the next 12 triangle numbers.

6 What do you notice about your answers to part **e**?

Coordinates

Look at the grid on the right.

We can describe the position of a point on the grid using a coordinate.

For example, the point A has a coordinate of (2, 3).

This is found by reading from the horizontal axis first and the vertical axis second. Similarly, the coordinate of B is (4, 4), the coordinate of C is (6, 2) and the coordinate of D is (3, 0).

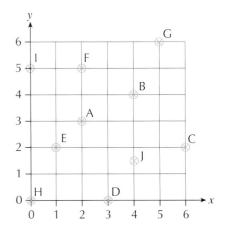

1 From the grid above, write down the coordinates of the points E, F, G, H, I and J.

2 Copy the grid above without the points marked on.

On your grid, draw the points with coordinates:

P(5, 2), Q(2, 4), R(3, 3), S(4, 0) and T(0, 5)

3 Look at the grid on the right.

a Write down the coordinates of A, B and C.

b ABC are three corners of a square.
Write down the coordinates of the 4th corner.

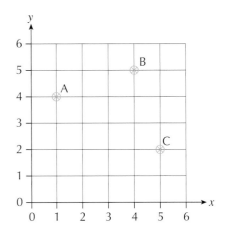

4 Look at the grid on the right.

a Write down the coordinates of L, M and N.

b LMN are three corners of a parallelogram.
Write down two possible coordinates for the position of the 4th corner.

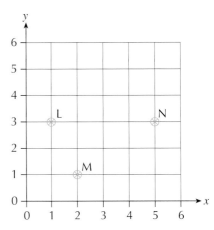

Look at the grid on the right.

The point *A* has a coordinate (4, –3).

The point *B* has a coordinate (–4, 4).

The point *C* has a coordinate (–5, –3).

Write down the coordinates of the points *D, E, F, G, H, I* and *J*.

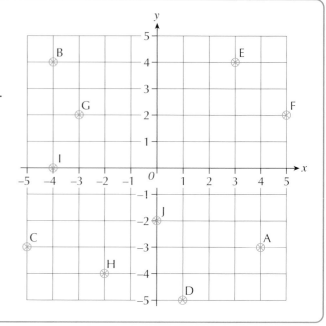

Naming graphs

When we use coordinates, we call the left-hand number the **x-coordinate** and the right-hand number the **y-coordinate**.

This means we can write a *general* coordinate pair as (x, y).

What do you notice about the coordinates (0, 3), (1, 3), (2, 3), (3, 3), (4, 3)?

The second number, the y-coordinate, is always 3. In other words, $y = 3$.

Look what happens when we plot it.

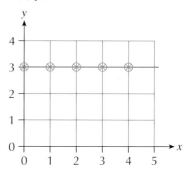

See also the graphs of $y = 2$ and $y = 5$, shown below.

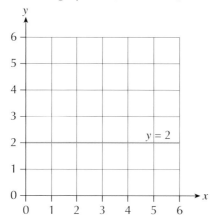

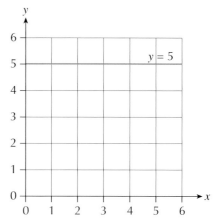

Note: the graphs are always horizontal lines for $y = A$, where A is any fixed number.

When we repeat this for an x-value, say $x = 2$, we get a vertical line, as shown.

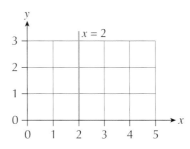

1 Write down the name of the straight line that goes through each of these pairs of points on the diagram.

a A and B   **b** C and D

c E and F   **d** G and H

e I and D   **f** J and D

g K and A   **h** G and F

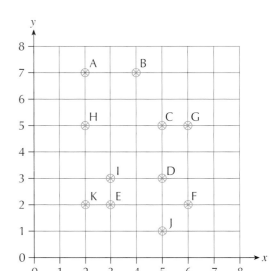

2 Draw each of the following graphs on the same grid, and label them.

a $y = 1$ **b** $y = 4$

c $y = 6$ **d** $x = 1$

e $x = 3$ **f** $x = 5$

Axes
x-axis from 0 to 7
y-axis from 0 to 7

3 Write down the letters that are on each of the following lines.

a $x = 1$ **b** $y = 1$

c $y = 6$ **d** $y = 2$

e $x = 3$ **f** $x = 2$

g $y = 4$ **h** $x = 5$

i $x = 6$ **j** $y = 3$

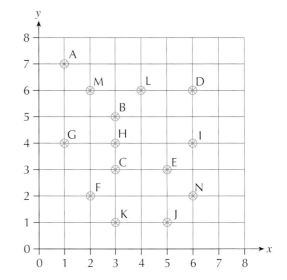

4 Draw each of the following pairs of lines on the same grid. Write down the coordinates of the point where they cross.

a $y = 1$ and $x = 3$

b $y = 4$ and $x = 1$

c $x = 5$ and $y = 6$

Here are eight pairs of coordinates:

A(2, 3)   B(3, 5)   C(7, 3)   D(2, 5)   E(3, 7)   F(7, 4)   G(3, 4)   H(7, 7)

Try to write down the names of the straight lines that the following points are on. Then plot the points on the graphs to check your answers.

a   A and C   **b**   B and D   **c**   C and F   **d**   A and D

e   E and H   **f**   F and G   **g**   B and G   **h**   C and H

From mappings to graphs

Think about the function ➝ +1 ➝ .

We can show this function in a diagram (right).

If we put the numbers together to form ordered pairs, we get:

(1, 2), (2, 3), (3, 4), (4, 5), (5, 6)

We have chosen just five starting points, but we could have chosen many more.

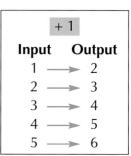

We can use these ordered pairs as coordinates, and plot them on a pair of axes, as shown on the right.

Notice how we use the first number to go along to the right, and the second number to go up. We can join up all the points with a straight line.

You can see from the mapping diagram that the Output = Input + 1.

As we plot the input along the x axis and the output along the y axis, we can write this as $y = x + 1$, which is the equation of the line.

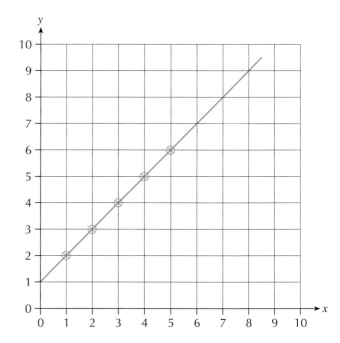

Exercise 11E

1 For each of the following:

   i   Complete the input/output diagram.

   ii   Complete the coordinates alongside.

   iii Plot the coordinates and draw the graph (use a grid like the one above).

   iv   Write down the equation of the line as $y = \boxed{}$

a

+ 2	Coordinates
0 ⟶ 2	(0, 2)
1 ⟶ 3	(1, 3)
2 ⟶	(2,)
3 ⟶	(3,)
4 ⟶	(4,)
5 ⟶	(5,)

b

× 2	Coordinates
0 ⟶ 0	(0, 0)
1 ⟶ 2	(1, 2)
2 ⟶	(2,)
3 ⟶	(3,)
4 ⟶	(4,)
5 ⟶	(5,)

c

÷ 2	Coordinates
0 ⟶ 0	(0, 0)
2 ⟶ 1	(2, 1)
4 ⟶	(4,)
6 ⟶	(6,)
8 ⟶	(8,)
10 ⟶	(10,)

d

+ 4	Coordinates
1 ⟶ 5	(1, 5)
2 ⟶ 6	(2, 6)
3 ⟶	(3,)
4 ⟶	(4,)
5 ⟶	(5,)
6 ⟶	(6,)

2 A special line is the one where the input is the same as the output. This can be represented by the mapping:

the same	Coordinates
0 ⟶ 0	(0, 0)
1 ⟶ 1	(1, 1)
2 ⟶	(2,)
3 ⟶	(3,)
4 ⟶	(4,)
5 ⟶	(5,)

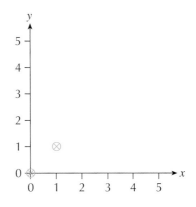

a Complete the mapping diagram.

b Use the coordinates to draw a graph on a copy of the grid.

This is the line $y = x$ because the x-coordinate is always the same as the y-coordinate.

This is an important line and one you should remember.

Extension **Work**

Write down pairs of values for x and y that are true for these equations (they do not have to be pairs of whole numbers).

Plot the values on a graph.

Describe anything you notice.

a $x + y = 6$ **b** $x + y = 8$ **c** $x + y = 3$

4

I can recognise the square numbers 1, 4, 9, 16, 25, etc.

I can recognise the triangular number pattern and the triangle numbers, 1, 3, 6, 10, 15, 21, …

I can continue the triangular number pattern for at least ten terms up to the triangle number 55.

I can read the position of and plot points from a grid.

5

I can work out and plot coordinates using a mapping diagram of an algebraic relationship such as $y = x + 2$, i.e.

$$2 \to 4$$
$$3 \to 5$$
$$4 \to 6$$

I can draw and recognise lines of the form $y = 3$ and $x = 2$, for example.

I can draw and recognise the line $y = x$.

I can read the position of and plot points from a grid using negative numbers.

National Test questions

1   *2000 Paper 2*

a   Write down the next two numbers in the sequence below.

| 1 | 4 | 9 | 16 | 25 | | |

b   Describe the pattern in part **a** in your own words.

2   *2003 3–5 Paper 2*

Some pupils throw two fair six-sided dice. Each die is numbered 1 to 6.
One die is blue. The other die is red.

Anna's dice show **blue 5, red 3**.
Her **total score** is **8**.
The cross on the grid shows her throw.

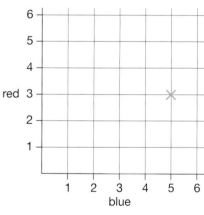

a   Carl's total score is 6.

Copy the grid below and put crosses on it to show **all** the different
pairs of numbers that Carl's dice could show.

b   The pupils play a game.

Winning rule: Win a point if the number on the **blue** die is **the same as**
the number on the **red** die.

Draw the grid again and put crosses on it to show all the different
winning throws.

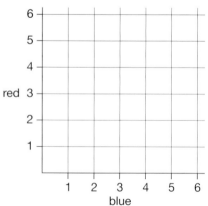

c The pupils play a different game.
This grid shows all the different winning throws.

Complete the sentence below to show the winning rule.

Winning rule: Win a point if the number on the blue die is ...

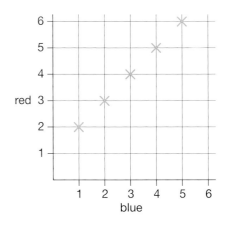

3 *2004 3-5 Paper 2*

I put square tiles on a large grid so that the tiles touch at the corners.
The diagram shows part of my diagonal pattern.

a The **bottom right-hand** corner of **tile 2** is marked with a •.

Write the coordinates of this point.

b **Tile 4** touches two other tiles.

Write the coordinates of the points where tile 4 touches two other tiles.

c Write the coordinates of the points where **tile 17** touches two other tiles.

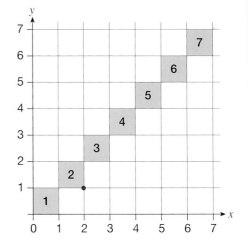

d I have **30 tiles** to make a pattern on a grid.
The pattern is a series of squares:
I have used some of the 30 tiles to make my pattern.

Do I have enough tiles left to make the **next square**, of side length 4?

Show your working to explain your answer.

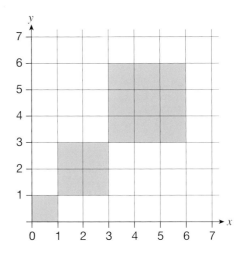

CHAPTER 12

Geometry and Measures **3**

This chapter is going to show you	What you should already know
● How to measure and draw angles ● How to construct triangles and other shapes ● How to use the geometrical properties of triangles and quadrilaterals	● How to recognise acute and obtuse angles ● How to draw and measure straight lines to the nearest millimetre

Measuring and drawing angles

Notice that on a semicircular protractor there are two scales. The outer scale goes from 0° to 180°, and the inner one goes from 180° to 0°. It is important that you use the correct scale.

When measuring or drawing an angle, always decide first whether it is an acute angle or an obtuse angle.

Acute angles are less than 90°.

Obtuse angles are greater than 90° but less than 180°.

Example 12.1 ▷ Measure the size of the angle shown on the right.

First, decide whether the angle to be measured is acute or obtuse. This is an acute angle (less than 90°).

Place the centre of the protractor at the corner of the angle, as in the diagram.

The two angles shown on the protractor scales are 60° and 120°. Since you are measuring an acute angle, the angle is 60° (to the nearest degree).

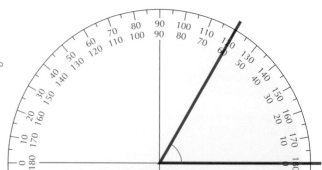

Example 12.2

Measure the size of this obtuse angle.

Place the centre of the protractor at the corner of the angle, as in the diagram.

The two angles shown on the protractor scales are 30° and 150°. Since you are measuring an obtuse angle, the angle is 150° (to the nearest degree).

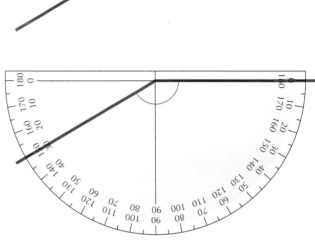

1. Measure the size of each of the following angles. Give your answers to the nearest degree.

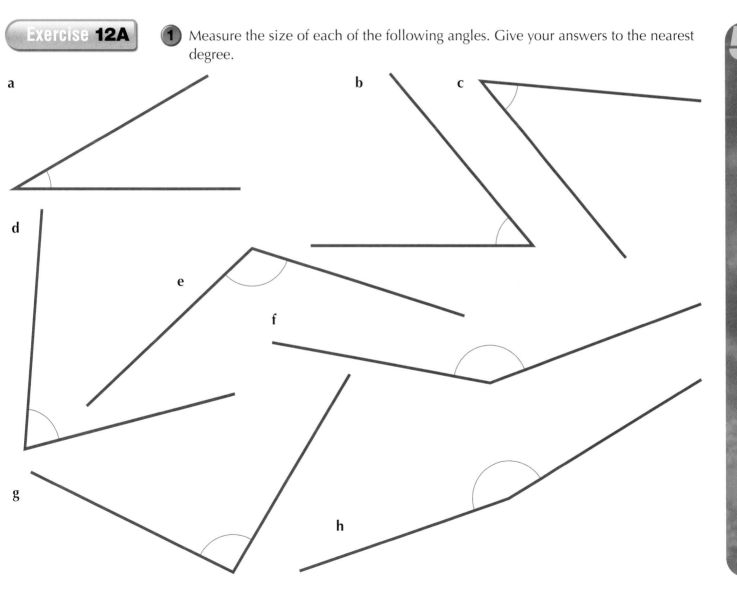

a

b   c

d

e

f

g

h

2 Draw and label each of the following angles.

a 20°	**b** 60°	**c** 80°	**d** 35°	**e** 57°
f 62°	**g** 100°	**h** 130°	**i** 145°	**j** 128°

3 a Measure the three angles in triangle ABC.
  b Add the three angles together.
  c Comment on your answer.

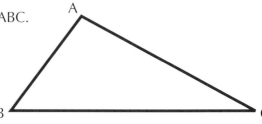

Estimating angles

- Copy the table below.

Angle	Estimate	Actual	Difference
1			
2			
3			
4			

- Estimate the size of each of the four angles below and complete the Estimate column in the table.

1  2 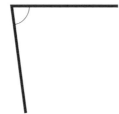 3  4

- Now measure the size of each angle to the nearest degree and complete the Actual column.
- Work out the difference between your estimate and the actual measurement for each angle and complete the Difference column.

Constructions

You need to be able to draw a shape exactly from length and angle information given on a diagram, using a ruler and a protractor. This is known as **constructing a shape**.

When constructing shapes you need to be accurate enough to draw the lines to the nearest millimetre and the angles to the nearest degree.

Example 12.3 ▷ Here is a sketch of a triangle ABC. It is not drawn accurately.

Construct the triangle ABC.
- Draw line BC 7 cm long.
- Draw an angle of 50° at B.
- Draw line AB 5 cm long.
- Join AC to complete the triangle.

The completed, full-sized triangle is given on the right.

Example 12.4 ▷ Here is a sketch of a triangle XYZ. It is not drawn accurately.

Construct the triangle XYZ.
- Draw line YZ 8 cm long.
- Draw an angle of 40° at Y.
- Draw an angle of 50° at Z.
- Extend both angle lines to intersect at X to complete the triangle.

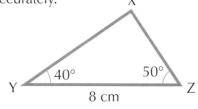

The completed, full-sized triangle is given on the right.

Exercise 12B

1 Construct each of the following triangles. Remember to label all lines and angles. The triangles are not drawn to scale.

a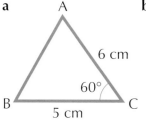

b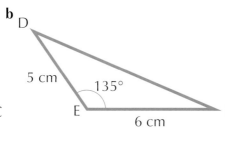

c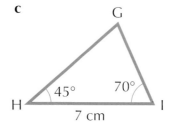

d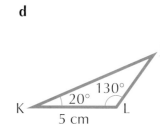

2   **a**   Construct the triangle PQR.
     b   Measure the size of ∠P and ∠R to
        the nearest degree.
     c   Measure the length of the line PR to
        the nearest millimetre.

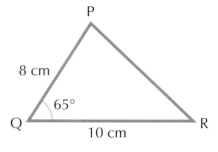

3   Construct the triangle ABC with
     ∠A = 100°, ∠B = 40° and AB = 7 cm.

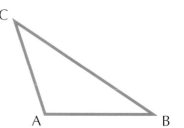

Extension   **Work**

Construct the following right-angled triangles.

1   **2**   **3**

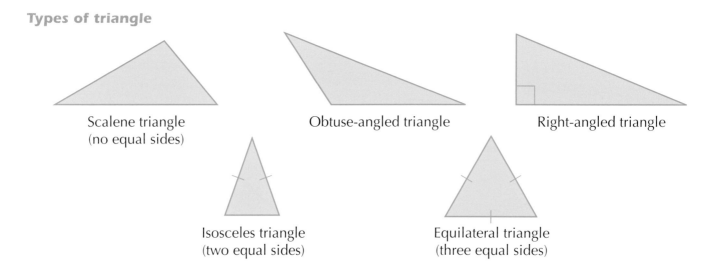

3 cm   5 cm   6 cm

4 cm   12 cm   8 cm

For each one, measure the length of the longest side.

Solving geometrical problems

Types of triangle

Scalene triangle
(no equal sides)

Obtuse-angled triangle

Right-angled triangle

Isosceles triangle
(two equal sides)

Equilateral triangle
(three equal sides)

Types of quadrilateral

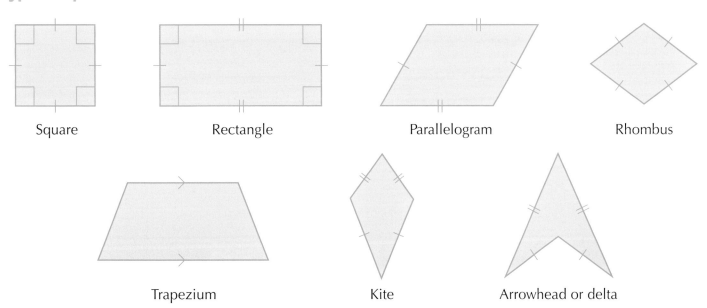

Square   Rectangle   Parallelogram   Rhombus

Trapezium   Kite   Arrowhead or delta

Exercise 12C

1 Which quadrilaterals have the following properties?

    a   Four equal sides   **b**   Two different pairs of equal sides

    c   Two pairs of parallel sides   **d**   Only one pair of parallel sides

2 Complete the following.

    a   A square is a special type of …

    b   A rectangle is a special type of …

    c   A rhombus is a special type of …

3 How many different triangles can be constructed on this 3 by 3 pin-board?

Use square dotted paper to record your triangles. Below each one, write down what type of triangle it is.

Here are two examples:

4 Copy this square on a piece of card. Then draw in the two diagonals and cut out the four triangles.

How many different triangles or quadrilaterals can you make using some or all of the triangles?

Make a copy of all the different shapes you have drawn.

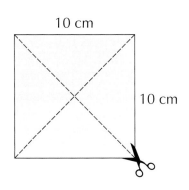

10 cm

10 cm

Extension Work

Here are six sticks:

2 cm	3 cm	4 cm

2 cm	3 cm	4 cm

How many different triangles or quadrilaterals can you make using these sticks? Use geosticks to help.

Make a copy of all the different shapes you have drawn.

LEVEL BOOSTER

4 I know the names of the different types of triangles and quadrilaterals.
I can solve problems about triangles and quadrilaterals.

5 I can draw and measure angles to the nearest degree.

National Test questions

1 *2000 Paper 2*

Look at this quadrilateral. Then make three copies of it.

You can draw one line on the quadrilateral to make two triangles.

a Use a ruler to draw a line in a different place on the quadrilateral to make two triangles.

b Now draw one line on the quadrilateral to make a quadrilateral and a triangle.

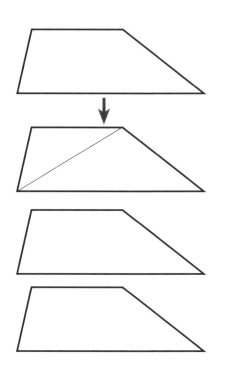

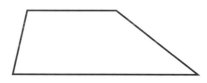

c Now draw one line on the quadrilateral to make two quadrilaterals.

d Copy the square on the right. Draw two lines on the square to make four triangles that are all the same size.

e Copy the square on the right. Now draw two lines on the square to make four squares that are all the same size.

Use a ruler and draw the squares accurately.

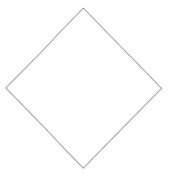

2 *2006 3–5 Paper 1*

a The line on the square grid on the right is one side of a **square**. Copy the diagram and draw 3 more lines to complete the square.

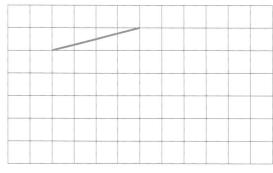

b The line on the square grid on the right is one side of a **quadrilateral**.

The quadrilateral has **only one pair of parallel sides**.

Copy the diagram and draw 3 more lines to show what the quadrilateral could be.

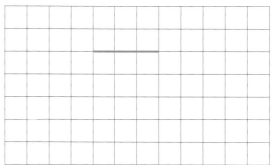

3 **a** Copy and complete the drawing to show an angle of 157°. Label the angle 157°.

b 15 pupils measured two angles. Here are their results.

A

Angle measured as	Number of pupils
36°	1
37°	2
38°	10
39°	2

B

Angle measured as	Number of pupils
45°	5
134°	3
135°	4
136°	3

Use the results to decide what each angle is most likely to measure.

Angle **A** is ...°

How did you decide?

Angle **B** is ...°

How did you decide?

This chapter is going to show you	**What you should already know**
● How to find simple percentages ● How to work out ratios ● How to solve problems using ratio	● The main equivalent fractions, percentages and decimals ● How to find 10% of a quantity ● Tables up to 10×10

Percentages

One of these labels is from a packet of porridge oats. The other is from a toffee cake.

Compare the percentages of protein, carbohydrates, fat and fibre.

PORRIDGE OATS	
Typical values	**per 100 g**
Energy	1555 kJ/ 372 kcal
Protein	7.5 g
Carbohydrates	71 g
Fat	6.0 g
Fibre	6.0 g
Sodium	0.3 g

TOFFEE CAKE	
Typical values	**per 100 g**
Energy	1421 kJ/ 340 kcal
Protein	2.9 g
Carbohydrates	39.1 g
Fat	19.1 g
Fibre	0.3 g
Sodium	0.2 g

Example 13.1 ▷ Without using a calculator, find: **a** 15% of £260 **b** 35% of 32

    a 15% = 10% + 5%

       So 15% of £260 is 26 + 13 = £39.

    b 35% = 10% + 10% + 10% + 10% − 5%

       So 35% of 32 is $4 \times 3.2 - 1.6 = 12.8 - 1.6 = 11.2$.

Example 13.2 ▷ Work out: **a** 5% of £190 **b** 65% of 75 eggs

    a $(5 \div 100) \times 190 = £9.50$

    b $(65 \div 100) \times 75 = 48.75 = 49$ eggs

Example 13.3 ▷ Which is greater, 40% of 560 or 60% of 390?

    $(40 \div 100) \times 560 = 224$ $(60 \div 100) \times 390 = 234$

    So 60% of 390 is greater.

Exercise 13A

1. Write each percentage as a combination of simple percentages. The first two have been done for you.

   a 15% = 10% + 5%   **b** 30% = 10% + 10% + 10%

   c 20%   **d** 90%

   e 35%   **f** 55%

   g 80%   **h** 60%

2. Write down or work out the equivalent percentage and decimal to each of these fractions.

   a $\frac{1}{2}$ **b** $\frac{1}{4}$ **c** $\frac{3}{4}$

3. Write down or work out the equivalent percentage and fraction to each of these decimals.

   a 0.1   **b** 0.5   **c** 0.3

4. Write down or work out the equivalent fraction and decimal to each of these percentages.

   a 20%   **b** 80%   **c** 90%

5. Use your answers to question 1 to work out each of the following.

   a 10% of 320   **b** 50% of 45   **c** 30% of 260   **d** 20% of 68

   e 10% of 12   **f** 30% of 280 **g** 50% of 36   **h** 90% of 206

6. Work out each of these.

   a 15% of £560   **b** 45% of 64 books   **c** 75% of 190 chairs

   d 35% of £212   **e** 65% of 996 pupils   **f** 55% of 120 buses

   g 40% of 109 plants   **h** 80% of 345 bottles   **i** 60% of 365 days

7. Which is bigger:

   a 45% of 68 or 35% of 92?   **b** 20% of £86 or 80% of £26?

Extension Work

The pie chart shows the percentage of each part of the porridge oats given in the label on page 153.

Match the labels to the key.
The first one is done for you.

| Carbohydrates | Fat |
| Sodium | Fibre |

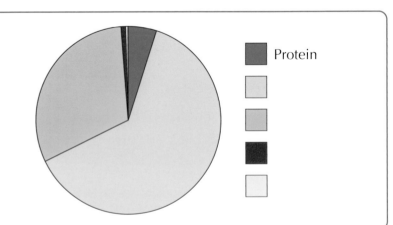

Protein

Ratio and proportion

Look at the fish tank. There are three types of fish – plain, striped and spotted.

What proportion of the fish are plain? What proportion are striped? What proportion are spotted?

Proportion is a way of comparing the parts of a quantity to the whole quantity.

Example 13.4 ▷ What proportion of this metre rule is shaded?

40 cm out of 100 cm are shaded. This is 40% (or 0.4 or $\frac{2}{5}$). This is 2 parts in every 5 parts.

Ratio of the shaded part to the unshaded part is 4 : 6 = 2 : 3.

Example 13.5 ▷ Look at the diagram below. What proportion of squares are black?

There is 1 black square for every 3 white squares. So, 1 in every 4 squares is black. This is 25% or $\frac{1}{4}$.

Exercise 13B

1 **i** For each of these metre rules, work out what proportion of the rule is shaded.

    ii For each rule, complete this statement:

        There are …… shaded parts in every 10 parts.

        This is …… in every ……

    a

    b

    c

    d

2 **i** For each bag of black and white balls over the page, work out what proportion of the balls are black.

    ii For each bag, complete this statement:

        There are …… black balls in …… balls in total.

        This is …… in every ……

a	b	c	d
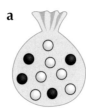	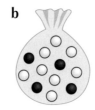	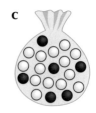	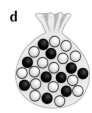

 3 Three bars of soap cost £1.80. How much would:

a 1 bar cost? **b** 12 bars cost? **c** 30 bars cost?

4 Look at the squares blow. 1 in every 5 squares is black.

Copy and fill in the table.

Number of black squares	Number of white squares
1	4
2	8
3	
5	
	32
	40

5 In the Eastlife fan club, there are 9 girls for every 1 boy.

a There are 50 boys in the club. How many girls are there?
b What proportion of the club is boys?

6 Tom and Jerry have some coins. This table shows the coins they have.

	1p	2p	5p	10p	20p	50p
Tom	10	20	20	10	30	10
Jerry	30	40	20	10	60	40

a How many coins does Tom have altogether?
b How many coins does Jerry have altogether?
c Copy and complete the table below, which shows the proportion of each coin that they have.

	1p	2p	5p	10p	20p	50p
Tom	10%					
Jerry	15%					

d Add up the proportions for Tom. Add up the proportions for Jerry. Explain your answers.

In the fish tank in the picture on page 155, there are 2 spotted fish and 8 striped fish. This means that there is 1 spotted fish for every 4 striped fish.

1   Copy and complete each of these statements:
   a   There is 1 spotted fish for every ...... plain fish.
   b   There are 4 striped fish for every ...... plain fish.

2   Now use the four bags of balls in Question 2.
   a   In bag a there are 2 black balls for every ...... white balls.
   b   In bag b there is 1 black ball for every ...... white balls.
   c   In bag c there are 3 black balls for every ...... white balls.
   d   In bag d there are 2 black balls for every ...... white balls.

   Comparisons like this are called ratios.

Calculating ratios and proportions

The fish have been breeding!

What is the ratio of striped fish to spotted fish?

What is the ratio of plain fish to spotted fish?

What is the ratio of plain fish to striped fish?

Ratio is a way of comparing the different parts of a quantity.

If five more plain fish are added to the tank, how many more striped fish would have to be added to keep the ratio of plain to striped the same?

Example 13.6   Reduce the following ratios to their simplest form : **a** $4:6$ **b** $5:25$

a   The highest common factor of 4 and 6 is 2. So, divide 2 into both values, giving $4:6 = 2:3$.

b   The highest common factor of 5 and 25 is 5. So, divide 5 into both values, giving $5:25 = 1:5$.

Example 13.7   A fruit drink is made by mixing 20 cl of orange juice with 60 cl of pineapple juice. What is the ratio of orange juice to pineapple juice?

Orange : pineapple = $20:60 = 1:3$ (cancel by 20)

Exercise 13C

1   Reduce each of the following ratios to its simplest form.
   a $4:8$ **b** $3:9$ **c** $2:10$ **d** $9:12$ **e** $5:20$ **f** $8:10$
   g $4:6$ **h** $10:15$ **i** $2:14$ **j** $4:14$ **k** $6:10$ **l** $25:30$

2   Write down the ratio of red : white from each of these metre rules.

   a

   b

3 There are 300 lights on a Christmas tree. 120 are white, 60 are blue, 45 are green and the rest are yellow.

Write down each of the following ratios in its simplest form.
- **a** white : blue
- **b** blue : green
- **c** green : yellow
- **d** white : blue : green : yellow

FM **4** To make jam, Josh uses strawberries and preserving sugar in the ratio 3 cups : 1 cup.

a How many cups of each will he need to make 20 cups of jam altogether?

b If he has 12 cups of strawberries, how many cups of sugar will he need?

c If he has $2\frac{1}{2}$ cups of sugar, how many cups of strawberries will he need?

Extension Work

FM

Proportion can be used to solve 'best buy' problems.

For example: a large tin of dog food costs £1 and contains 500 grams.

A small tin costs 50p and contains 300 grams. Which tin is the better value?

For each tin, work out how much 1 gram costs. (You will need a calculator.)

Large tin: 500 ÷ 100 = 5 grams per penny
Small tin: 300 ÷ 50 = 6 grams per penny

So, the small tin is the better buy.

Always divide the quantity by the amount of money.

1 A bottle of shampoo costs £2.70 and contains 30 cl. A different bottle of the same shampoo costs £1.50 and contains 20 cl. Which is the better buy?

2 A large roll of sticky tape has 75 metres of tape and costs 75p. A small roll of the same tape has 20 metres of tape and costs 40p. Which roll is better value?

3 A pad of A4 paper costs £2.40 and has 120 sheets. A thicker pad of A4 paper costs £1.50 and has 150 sheets. Which pad is the better buy?

4 A small tin of peas contains 250 grams and costs 34p. A large tin contains 500 grams and costs 60p. Which tin is the better buy?

Find the costs and quantities of different items in your local supermarket.
Draw up a table or make a poster of 'best buys'.

Solving problems

A painter has a 4-litre can of blue paint and 2 litres of yellow paint in a 4-litre can (Picture 1).

Picture 1   **Picture 2**   **Picture 3**

He pours 2 litres of blue paint into the other can (Picture 2) and mixes it thoroughly.

He then pours 1 litre from the second can back into the first can (Picture 3) and mixes it thoroughly.

How much blue paint is in the first can now?

Example 13.8 Divide £50 in the ratio 3 : 7.

There are 3 + 7 = 10 portions. This gives £50 ÷ 10 = £5 per portion. So, one share of the £50 is 3 × £5 = £15, and the other share is 7 × £5 = £35.

Example 13.9 Divide £150 in the ratio 1 : 5.

There are 1 + 5 = 6 portions. This gives £150 ÷ 6 = £25 per portion. So one share of the £150 is 1 × 25 = £25, and the other share is 5 × £25 = £125.

Exercise 13D

1 In the pattern below, 1 square in every 4 is black. The proportion of black squares is $\frac{1}{4}$.

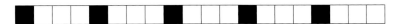

a What is the proportion of white squares?

b Copy and complete the table.

Black squares	White squares	Total squares
1	3	4
2	6	
8		
20		
		90

c If you know the number of black squares, how would you work out the number of white squares?

d If you know the number of white squares, how would you work out the number of black squares?

e If you know the total number of squares, how would you work out the number of black squares and the number of white squares?

FM 2 Billy is mixing blue and yellow paint to make green paint. For every can of blue paint, he needs two cans of yellow paint.

a If he has two cans of blue paint, how many cans of yellow paint will he need?

b If he has 10 cans of yellow paint, how many cans of blue paint will he need?

c He needs 12 cans of green paint. How many cans of blue paint and of yellow paint will he need?

3 Divide £100 in each of these ratios below.

a 1 : 4   b 1 : 9   c 1 : 3

4 There are 360 pupils in a primary school. The ratio of girls to boys is 2:1. How many boys and girls are there in the school?

5 Freda has 120 CDs. The ratio of pop CDs to dance CDs is 5:1. How many of each type of CD are there?

6 Mr Smith has 24 calculators in a box. The ratio of ordinary calculators to scientific calculators is 5:1. How many of each type of calculator does he have?

7 **a** There are 15 bottles on the wall. The ratio of green bottles to brown bottles is 1:4. How many green bottles are there on the wall?

   b One green bottle accidentally falls. What is the ratio of green to brown bottles now?

Extension Work

Uncle Fred has decided to give his nephew and niece, Jack and Jill, £100 between them. He decides to split the £100 in the ratio of their ages. Jack is 4 and Jill is 6. You will need a calculator for this.

a How much do each get?

b The following year he does the same thing with another £100. Jack is now 5 and Jill is 7. How much do each get now? (Give you answer to the nearest penny.)

c He does this for another 3 years. Work out how much Jack and Jill each get each year.

LEVEL BOOSTER

3 I can use simple additions to build up percentages.

4 I can recognise simple proportions of a whole and describe them using fractions or percentages.
I can work out simple percentages.

5 I can write down and simplify ratios.
I can calculate a percentage of a quantity.

6 I can divide a quantity in a given ratio.

National Test questions

1 *2004 3–5 Paper 2*

The pie charts show what percentage of household rubbish is recycled in different countries.

England	Germany	Norway	Spain
	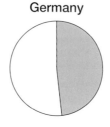		

a In England, about what percentage is recycled?

b England wants to recycle 30% of its rubbish by the year 2010.

Which countries already recycle more than 30% of their rubbish?

Key

◻ (grey) % of rubbish recycled   ◻ (white) % of rubbish not recycled

 2 *2004 4–6 Paper 2*

Here are the ingredients for a cordial used to make a drink.

> 50 g ginger
> 1 lemon
> 1.5 litres of water
> 900 g sugar

a Jenny is going to make this cordial with **25 g** of ginger.

How much lemon, water and sugar should she use?

> 25 g ginger
> … lemon
> … litres of water
> … g sugar

b The finished drink should be $\frac{1}{3}$ cordial and $\frac{2}{3}$ water. Jenny puts **100 ml** of cordial in a glass.

How much water should she put with it?

3 *2005 4–6 Paper 1*

a Complete these sentences:

◻ out of 10 is the same as 70%.   10 out of 20 is the same as ◻ %

b Complete the sentence:

◻ out of ◻ is the same as 5%

Now complete the sentence again using **different** numbers.

 4 *2006 4–6 Paper 1*

a Work out the missing values:

10% of 84 = ◻   5% of 84 = ◻ $2\frac{1}{2}$% of 84 = ◻

b The cost of a CD player is £84 plus $17\frac{1}{2}$% tax.

What is the **total** cost of the CD player?

You can use part **a** to help you.

FM Smoothie bar

Small	300 ml	£2
Medium	400 ml	£3
Large	600 ml	£4

Fruity Surprise

100 g mango
50 g strawberries
75 g bananas
250 ml orange juice

Tropical Fruit

250 g tropical fru
100 ml yoghurt
85 g raspberries
½ lime juice
1 tsp honey

To make a small smoothie:
Use half of the ingredients in the medium recipe.

To make a large smoothie:
Just add 200 ml of fruit juice or milk.

1 Work out the recipe for a small Fruity Surprise.

2 Work out the recipe for a large Chocolate.

3 How much milk would be needed to make 50 small Breakfast Boost smoothies? Give the answer in litres.

6 How much cranberry juice is in a small Chocolate?

7 I am buying 10 small smoothies and 5 medium smoothies. How much will they cost without the offer?

8 If I buy one medium smoothie and one large smoothie, how much will I save using the offer?

This chapter is going to show you
- How to solve different types of problem using algebra

What you should already know
- Understand the rules of algebra
- How to use letters in place of numbers
- How to solve equations

Solving 'brick wall' problems

Example 14.1 ▷ The numbers in two 'bricks' which are side by side (adjacent) are added together. The answer is written in the 'brick' above. Find the number missing from the 'brick' in the bottom layer.

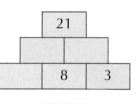

Let the missing number be x. This gives the second diagram on the right.

Adding the terms in all adjacent 'bricks' gives:
$$(x + 8) + 11 = 21$$
$$x + 19 = 21$$
$$x = 21 - 19 \text{ (Take 19 from both sides)}$$
$$x = 2$$

So, the missing number is 2.

Exercise 14A Find the unknown number x in each of these 'brick wall' problems.

1

2

3

4

5

6

7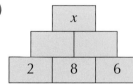

8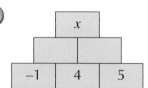

9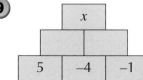

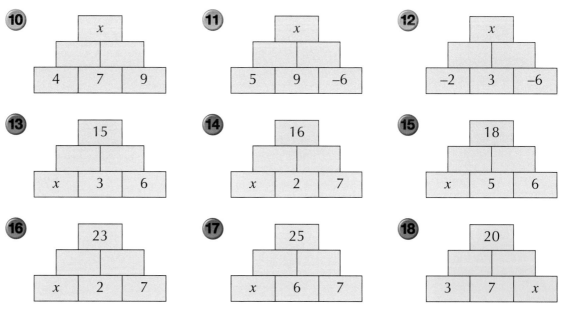

10

	x	
4	7	9

11

	x	
5	9	−6

12

	x	
−2	3	−6

13

	15	
x	3	6

14

	16	
x	2	7

15

	18	
x	5	6

16

	23	
x	2	7

17

	25	
x	6	7

18

	20	
3	7	x

Extension Work

1 Find the value of x in each of these.

a

	30	
5	x	3

b

	27	
2x	3	7

c

	21	
2x	5	3

d

	25	
5	7	2x

2 Make up some of your own 'brick wall' problems.

Solving square-and-circle problems

The number in each square is the sum of the numbers in the two circles on either side of the square.

Example 14.2

The values of A, B, C and D are positive, whole numbers. Work out the values of each of them.

From the diagram, write down the four equations for A, B, C and D. Then solve them in turn.

$A + 4 = 9$ shows that $A = 5$

$B + A = 12$
$B + 5 = 12$ shows that $B = 7$

$C + B = 9$
$C + 7 = 9$ shows that $C = 2$

$D = C + 4$
$D = 2 + 4$ shows that $D = 6$

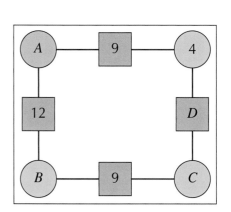

Example 14.3 ▷

A, B, C, D and E are numbers.

a When $A = 1$, write down the values of B, C, D and E.

b When $A = 2$, write down the values of B, C, D and E.

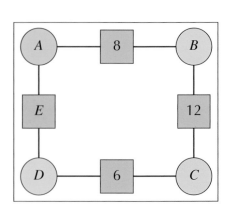

a When $A = 1$:

$B + 1 = 8$, so $B = 7$
$7 + C = 12$, so $C = 5$
$5 + D = 6$, so $D = 1$
$1 + 1 = E$, so $E = 2$

b When $A = 2$:

$2 + B = 8$, so $B = 6$
$6 + C = 12$, so $C = 6$
$6 + D = 6$, so $D = 0$
$0 + 2 = E$, so $E = 2$

Exercise 14B

1 Find the values of A, B, C and D in each of these square-and-circle puzzles.

a
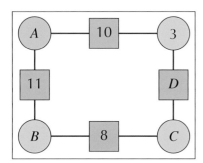

b
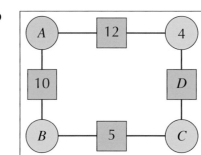

c
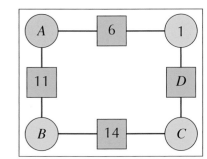

2 Find the values of A, B, C and D in each of these square-and-circle puzzles.

a
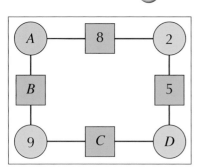

b
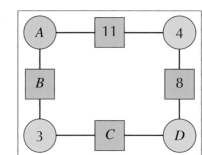

c
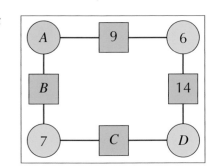

3 Find the solution set to each of the following square and circle puzzles for the value of *A* stated.

a
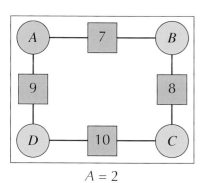
A = 2

b
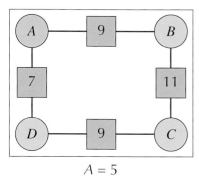
A = 3

c
A = 5

4 Find the solution set to each of the following square and circle puzzles for the value of *A* stated.

a
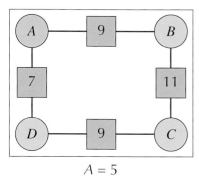
A = 5

b
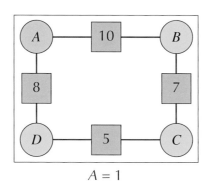
A = 1

c
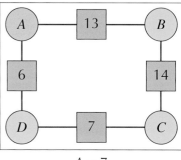
A = 7

Extension Work

1 Triangular square-and-circle problems only have one solution.
Find the values that fit in the circle for these triangles.

Hint: Guess a value for A, work out B and C, then check that they all work.

a
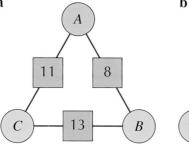

b
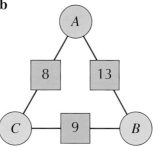

c
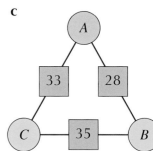

2 What is the connection between the sum of the squares and the sum of the circles?

4 I can solve a problem using algebra, such as finding the value of x in this 'brick wall' problem.

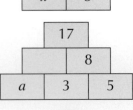

5 I can solve a simple problem using simple algebra, such as finding the value of a in this 'brick wall' problem.

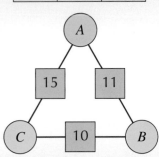

I can solve a mathematical problem such as the triangle-and-circle problem below, using trial and improvement.

National Test questions

1 *2000 Paper 1*

Copy the number triangle on the right.

Make each side of the triangle add up to 900.

Use these numbers

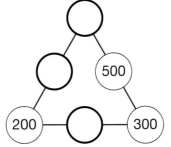

2 *2004 3–5 Paper 1*

This question is about number pyramids.
You **add two numbers** to work out the number that goes on top of them.

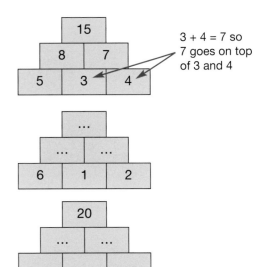

3 + 4 = 7 so
7 goes on top
of 3 and 4

a Copy and complete the number pyramid below.

b Copy and complete the number pyramid below in two **different** ways.

3 *2000 Paper 1*

Here is a number triangle.

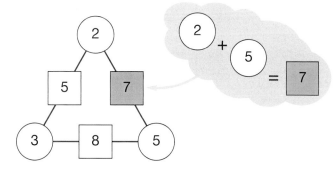

You will find the number in a square by adding the numbers in the two circles on either side of it.

Look at the following number triangles.

Copy the triangles and fill in the missing numbers.

a

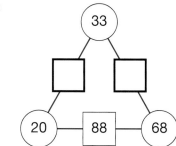

b

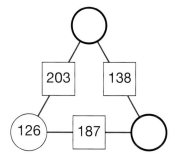

Child trust fund

Use the information in the child trust funds key to answer the following questions.

Child trust fund

- Children born on or after 1 September 2002 get a £250 voucher from the government to start their child trust fund account.
- They get a further payment of £250 from the government on their seventh birthday.
- If the household income is below the Child Tax Credit income threshold they get an additional £250 with each payment.
- Parents, relatives and friends can contribute a maximum of £1200 a year between them to the fund.
- All interest or earnings on the account is tax-free.
- The child (and no-one else) can withdraw the money in the fund when they are 18.
- Money cannot be taken out of the account until the child is 18.

Average annual growth 3%										
		Average annual investment								
		0	150	300	450	600	750	900	1050	1200
Potential amount in account after years shown	1	258	408	558	708	858	1008	1158	1308	1458
	7	565	1714	2864	4013	5162	6312	7461	8611	9760
	13	675	3017	5360	7703	10045	12388	14731	17073	19416
	18	782	4294	7806	11319	14831	18343	21855	25367	28879

Average annual growth 6%										
		Average annual investment								
		0	150	300	450	600	750	900	1050	1200
Potential amount in account after years shown	1	265	415	565	715	865	1015	1165	1315	1465
	7	641	1900	3159	4418	5677	6936	8195	9454	10714
	13	909	3741	6574	9406	12238	15071	17903	20735	23568
	18	1217	5852	10488	15124	19760	24396	29032	33668	38303

1.
   a What is 5% of £250?
   b What is 1% of £250?
   c What is 2% of £250?
   d What is 3% of £250?

2. Would a child born on the 22nd August 2002 be entitled to the government grant of £250? If not, why?

3. What is the maximum amount that parents, relatives and friends can invest in the account each year?

4. If the average annual growth rate is 3% and an average of £300 is invested each year, how much would be in the account when the child is 18 years old?

5. If the average annual growth rate is 6% and an average of £900 is invested each year, how much would be in the account when the child is 18 years old?

6. A family has an income below the Child Tax Credit limit. They invest an average of £150 in the child trust fund at an average growth rate of 3%. Approximately how much will be in the account when the child is 18?

7. If the annual average growth rate had been 3% and at the age of 18 a child had approximately £18 000 in their trust fund, how much was the average annual investment?

8. If a child lived in a household where the income was below the Child Tax Credit limit and no extra investment was made into the fund, explain why there would be approximately £1564 in the trust fund after 18 years.

9. Look at the amounts in the accounts after 1 year.
   a By how much do the amounts increase for both the average growth rates of 3% and 6%?
   b How much would be in the account after 1 year if the average growth rate is 3% and the amount invested is £75?
   c How much would be in the account after 1 year if the average growth rate is 6% and the amount invested is £675?

Line symmetry

A 2-D shape has a **line of symmetry** when one half of the shape fits exactly over the other half when the shape is folded along that line.

A mirror or tracing paper can be used to check whether a shape has a line of symmetry. Some shapes have no lines of symmetry while others have more than one.

A line of symmetry is also called a **mirror line**.

Example 15.1 ▷

This T-shape has one line of symmetry, as shown.

Put a mirror on the line of symmetry and check that the image in the mirror is half the T-shape.

Next, trace the T-shape and fold the tracing along the line of symmetry to check that both halves of the shape fit exactly over each other.

Example 15.2 ▷

This cross has four lines of symmetry, as shown.

Check that each line drawn here is a line of symmetry. Use either a mirror or tracing paper.

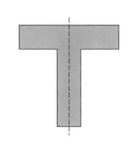

Example 15.3 ▷

This L-shape has no lines of symmetry.

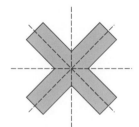

For this exercise, you may find tracing paper or a mirror helpful.

1 Copy each of these shapes and draw its lines of symmetry. Write below each shape the number of lines of symmetry it has.

a   b   c   d    e   f

Isosceles triangle   Equilateral triangle   Square   Rectangle   Parallelogram   Kite

2 Write down the number of lines of symmetry for each of the following shapes.

a   b   c   d

e   f   g   h

3 Write down the number of lines of symmetry for each of these road signs.

a    b   c   d   e    f

Extension **Work**

1 Sports logo

Design a logo for a new sports and leisure centre that is due to open soon. Your logo should have four lines of symmetry.

2 Flags

The flags of many countries are symmetrical. How many flags can you find which have line symmetry?

Rotational symmetry

A 2-D shape has **rotational symmetry** when it can be rotated about a point to look exactly the same in a new position.

The **order of rotational symmetry** tells you the number of different positions in which the shape looks the same when you rotate it by one complete turn (360°).

If you have to rotate a shape through a complete turn before it looks the same, then it has no rotational symmetry. We say its order of rotational symmetry is 1.

To find the order of rotational symmetry of a shape, use tracing paper.

- First, trace the shape.
- Then rotate the tracing paper until the tracing again fits exactly over the shape.
- Count the number of times that the tracing fits exactly over the shape until you return to the starting position.
- The number of times that the tracing fits is the order of rotational symmetry.

Example 15.4 ▷ This shape has rotational symmetry of order 3.

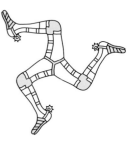

Example 15.5 ▷ This shape has rotational symmetry of order 4.

Example 15.6 ▷ This shape has no rotational symmetry.
Therefore, it has rotational symmetry of order 1.

Exercise 15B For this exercise, you may find the use of tracing paper is helpful.

1. Copy each of these capital letters and write below its order of rotational symmetry.

  a **H** b **M** c **N** d **S** e **W** f **X**

2. Write down the order of rotational symmetry for each of the shapes below.

  a   b   c d   e   f

3. Copy and complete the table for each of the following regular polygons.

  a   b   c  d 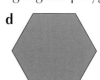 e

Shape	Number of lines of symmetry	Order of rotational symmetry
a Equilateral triangle		
b Square		
c Regular pentagon		
d Regular hexagon		
e Regular octagon		

What do you notice?

Reflections

The picture shows an L-shape reflected in a mirror.

You can draw the picture without the mirror, as follows.

The **object** is reflected in the mirror line to give the **image**. The mirror line becomes a line of symmetry. So, if the paper is folded along the mirror line, the object will fit exactly over the image. The image is the same distance from the mirror line as the object is.

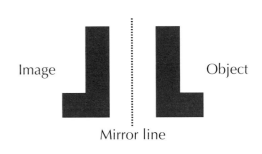

A reflection is an example of a **transformation**. A transformation is a way of changing the position or the size of a shape.

Example 15.7 ▷ Reflect this shape in the given mirror line.

Notice that the image is the same size as the object, and that the mirror line becomes a line of symmetry.

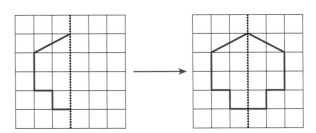

Example 15.8 ▷ Triangle A'B'C' is the reflection of triangle ABC in the given mirror line.

Notice that the point A and the point A' are the same distance from the mirror line, and that the line joining A and A' crosses the mirror line at 90°. This is true for all corresponding points on the object and its image.

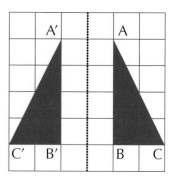

Example 15.9 ▷ Reflect this rectangle in the mirror line shown.

Use tracing paper or a mirror to check the reflection.

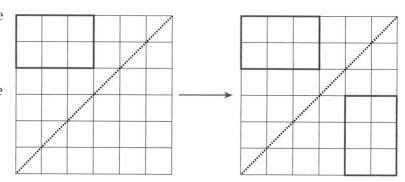

Exercise 15C For this exercise, you may find tracing paper or a mirror helpful.

1. Copy each of these diagrams onto squared paper and draw its reflection in the given mirror line.

   a   b   c   d

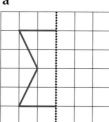 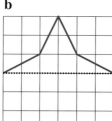 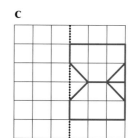 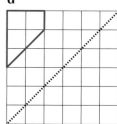

2. Copy each of these shapes onto squared paper and draw its reflection in the given mirror line.

   a   b   c   d

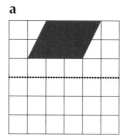 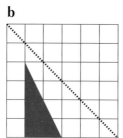 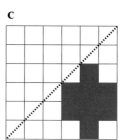 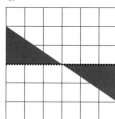

3 The points A(1, 2), B(2, 5), C(4, 4) and D(6, 1) are shown on the grid.

 a Copy the grid onto squared paper and plot the points A, B, C and D. Draw the mirror line.

 b Reflect the points in the mirror line and label them A′, B′, C′ and D′.

 c Write down the coordinates of the image points.

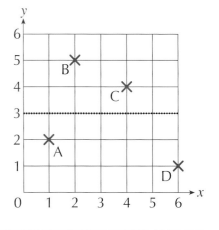

Extension Work

1 a Copy the diagram onto squared paper and reflect the triangle in mirror A. Now reflect the image you got in mirror B. Finally, reflect this image in mirror C.

 b Make up your own patterns using a series of parallel mirrors.

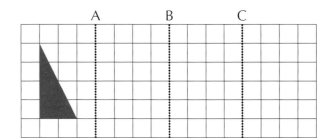

2 a Copy the grid on the right onto centimetre squared paper.

 b Reflect the shape in mirror line 1. Then reflect the new shape in mirror line 2.

 c Make up your own patterns using two perpendicular mirrors.

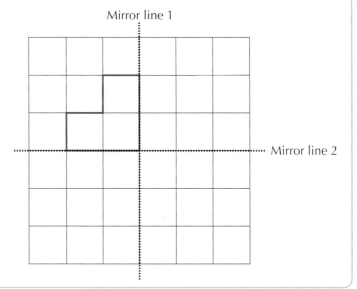

Rotations

Another type of transformation in geometry is **rotation**.

To describe the rotation of a 2-D shape, three facts must be known:
- **Centre of rotation** – the point about which the shape rotates.
- **Angle of rotation** – this is usually 90° ($\frac{1}{4}$ turn), 180° ($\frac{1}{2}$ turn) or 270° ($\frac{3}{4}$ turn).
- **Direction of rotation** – clockwise or anticlockwise.

When you rotate a shape, it is a good idea to use tracing paper.

As with reflections, the starting shape is called the object, and the rotated shape is called the image.

Example 15.10 ▷ The flag is rotated through 90° clockwise about the point X.

Notice that this is the same as rotating the flag through 270° anticlockwise about the point X.

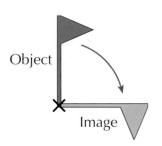

Object

Image

Example 15.11 ▷ This right-angled triangle is rotated through 180° clockwise about the point X.

Notice that rotating through 180° clockwise is always the same as rotating through 180° anticlockwise.

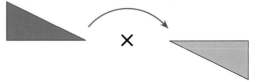

Example 15.12 ▷ △ABC has been rotated to △A'B'C' by a rotation of 90° anticlockwise about the point X.

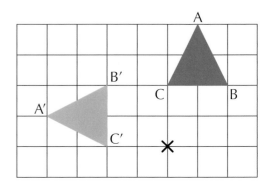

Exercise 15D For this exercise, you may find tracing paper helpful.

1. Copy each of the flags below and draw the image after each flag has been rotated about the point marked X through the angle indicated.

   a   **b**   **c**   **d**

   90° anticlockwise   180° clockwise   90° clockwise   270° anticlockwise

2. Copy each of the shapes below onto a square grid. Draw the image after each one has been rotated about the point marked X through the angle indicated.

a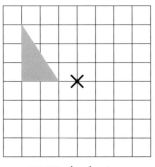

180° clockwise

b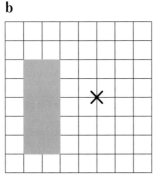

90° anticlockwise

c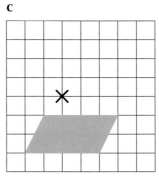

180° anticlockwise

d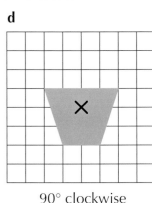

90° clockwise

1 Rotate the rectangle ABCD through 90° clockwise about the point (1,2) to give the image A'B'C'D'.

2 Write down the coordinates of A', B', C' and D'.

3 Which coordinate point remains fixed throughout the rotation?

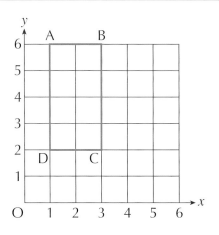

Translations

A translation is the movement of a 2-D shape from one position to another without reflecting it or rotating it.

The distance and direction of the translation are given by the number of unit squares moved to the right or left, followed by the number of unit squares moved up or down.

As with reflections and rotations, the original shape is called the object, and the translated shape is called the image.

Example 15.13

Triangle A has been translated to triangle B by a translation 3 units right, followed by 2 units up.

When an object is translated onto its image, every point on the object moves the same distance, as shown by the arrows.

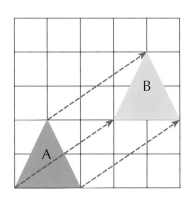

Example 15.14

The rectangle ABCD has been translated to rectangle A'B'C'D' by a translation 3 units left, followed by 3 units down.

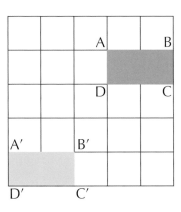

Exercise 15E

1 Describe each of the following translations:

   a from A to B

   b from A to C

   c from A to D

   d from A to E

   e from B to D

   f from C to E

   g from D to E

   h from E to A

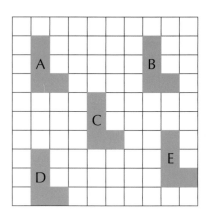

2 Copy the triangle ABC onto squared paper. Label it P.

   a Write down the coordinates of the vertices of triangle P.

   b Translate triangle P 6 units left and 2 units down. Label the new triangle Q.

   c Write down the coordinates of the vertices of triangle Q.

   d Translate triangle Q 5 units right and 4 units down. Label the new triangle R.

   e Write down the coordinates of the vertices of triangle R.

   f Describe the translation which translates triangle R onto triangle P.

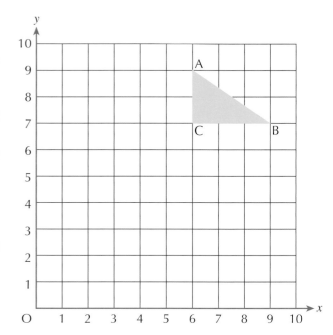

Extension Work

Use squared dotty paper or a pin-board for this investigation.

1 How many different translations of the triangle are possible on this 3 by 3 grid?

2 How many different translations of this triangle are possible on a 4 by 4 grid?

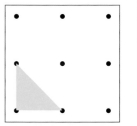

3 I can draw lines of symmetry on 2-D shapes.

4 I can reflect 2-D shapes in a mirror line.

5 I can find the order of rotational symmetry of a 2-D shape.
I can rotate a 2-D shape about a point of rotation.
I can translate a 2-D shape on a grid.

National Test questions

1 *2006 3–5 Paper 1*

The shapes below are drawn on square grids.

Each shape has **one line of symmetry**.

Copy the shapes and draw the line of symmetry on each shape.

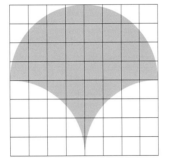 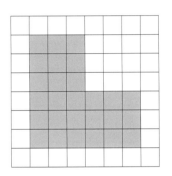

2 *2004 3–5 Paper 2*

'Windmill' patterns look the **same** when you **turn** the grid through one or more right angles.

Example:

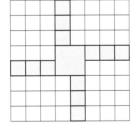

a **Shade 3 squares** to complete the windmill pattern on the square grid shown right.

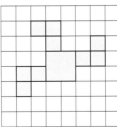

b **Shade 6 squares** to complete the windmill pattern on the square grid shown right.

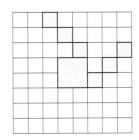

3 *2004 3–5 Paper 1*

Three different shapes are folded along a line of symmetry. For each shape, the **dashed line** is the **fold line**.

For each shape, draw what the shape looked like **before** it was folded.

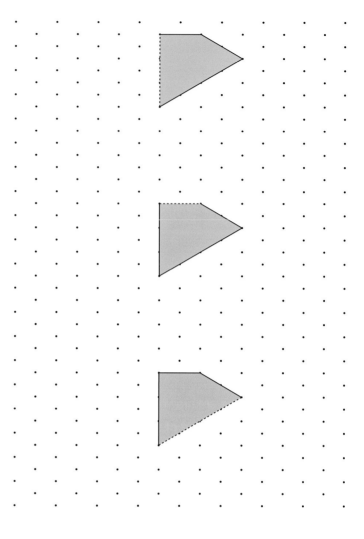

4 *2006 3–5 Paper 2*

The square grid shows a rectangle reflected in **two mirror lines**.

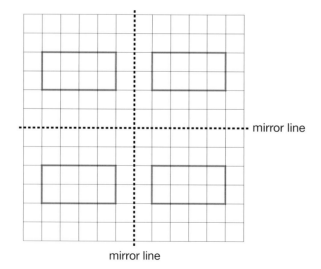

mirror line

mirror line

Copy the square grid below and show the triangle reflected in the two mirror lines.

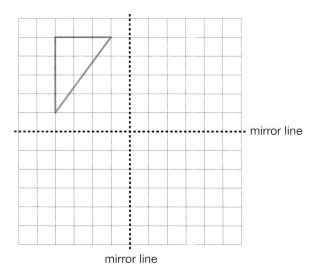

---------- mirror line

mirror line

5   *2005 3–5 Paper 1*

The shapes below are drawn on square grids.

The diagrams show a rectangle that is rotated, then rotated again.

The centre of rotation is marked •.

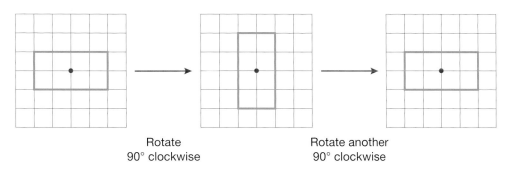

Rotate
90° clockwise

Rotate another
90° clockwise

On a copy of the grids below, complete the diagrams to show the triangle when it is rotated, then rotated again.

The centre of rotation is marked •.

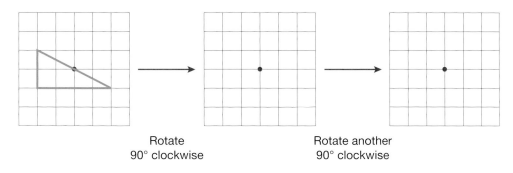

Rotate
90° clockwise

Rotate another
90° clockwise

Landmark spotting

Look at the symmetry of these famous landmarks

d The Angel of the North

1 How many lines of symmetry does each picture have?

Draw sketches to show the lines of symmetry.

a Notre Dame Cathedral

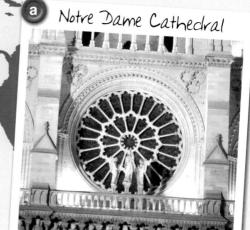

2 The picture for some of the buildings will have a different number of lines if the picture was taken directly from above.

How many lines of symmetry would a picture of the Eiffel Tower have if it was taken from above?

Draw a sketch to show the lines of symmetry.

3 The window on the picture of Notre Dame Cathedral also has line symmetry.

Design a window of your own that has line symmetry.

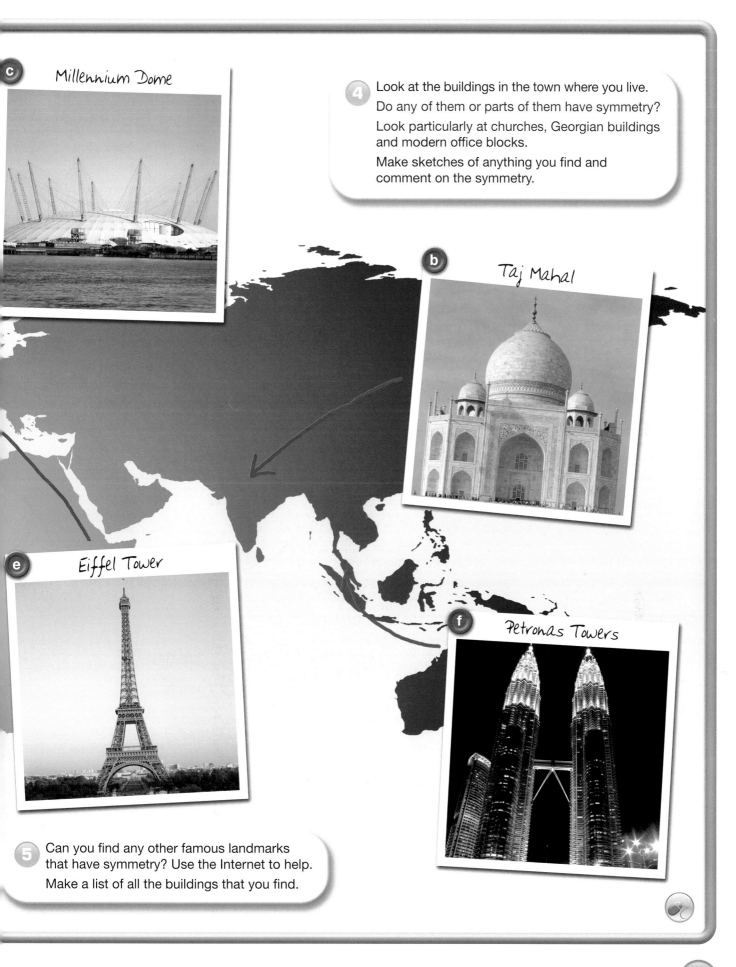

c Millennium Dome

4 Look at the buildings in the town where you live.

Do any of them or parts of them have symmetry?

Look particularly at churches, Georgian buildings and modern office blocks.

Make sketches of anything you find and comment on the symmetry.

b Taj Mahal

e Eiffel Tower

f Petronas Towers

5 Can you find any other famous landmarks that have symmetry? Use the Internet to help.

Make a list of all the buildings that you find.

<table>
<tr><td>

This chapter is going to show you

- How to draw a pie chart where the data are given as percentages
- How to find the median and the mean of a set of data
- How to carry out statistical surveys

</td><td>

What you should already know

- How to find the mode and the range of a set of data
- How to find experimental probability

</td></tr>
</table>

Pie charts

Sometimes information is given as a table of percentages. To draw pie charts using such data, you need to use a pie with ten sectors or divisions, like the one shown below.

Example 16.1 ▷ The table shows the favourite drinks of pupils in Year 7.

Draw a pie chart to show the data.

Milk	30%
Coke	40%
Coffee	20%
Tea	10%

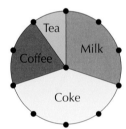

Milk is 30%. This means that Milk gets 3 divisions (each division = 10%), Coke gets 4 divisions, and so on.

Make sure the chart is labelled.

Example 16.2 ▷ The two tables below show the lateness of trains in Britain and Spain. Draw pie charts to show both sets of data. Write a sentence to compare the punctuality of trains in both countries.

Lateness: Britain	Percentage
On time	55
Up to 5 minutes late	10
Between 5 and 10 minutes late	15
More than 10 minutes late	20

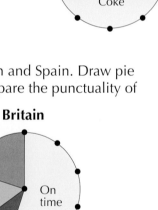

Lateness: Spain	Percentage
On time	85
Up to 5 minutes late	10
Between 5 and 10 minutes late	5
More than 10 minutes late	0

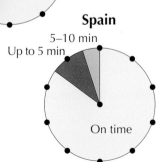

Each division on the pie represents 10%.

A greater percentage of trains in Spain are on time.

Exercise 16A

For each of the pie charts, start with a copy of the circle that is divided into ten sectors. Remember to label your pie chart.

1 Draw a pie chart to show the data in each table.

a Colours of cars in a car park

Colour	% of cars
Red	20%
Blue	30%
Green	20%
Yellow	10%
Black	20%

b Pets of Year 7 pupils

Pet	% of pets
Dog	30%
Cat	20%
Bird	10%
Fish	10%
Gerbil	30%

c Favourite subjects of Year 11 pupils

Subject	% of students
Maths	45
English	15
Geography	20
History	10
Games	10

d Favourite soap operas of Year 7 pupils

Soap opera	% of students
Eastenders	60
Coronation St	20
Emmerdale	10
Brookside	10

e Percentage distribution of age groups in Rotherham

Age	% of population
Under 16	15
16–25	20
26–40	30
41–60	20
Over 60	15

f Percentage distribution of age groups in Eastbourne

Age	% of population
Under 16	10
16–25	15
26–40	25
41–60	20
Over 60	30

 2 Write a sentence about the difference in the age distributions between Rotherham, which is an industrial city in the north of England, and Eastbourne, which is a seaside town on the south coast.

Extension Work

Find data that are given as percentages. For example, the table of constituents on the side of a cereal packet.

Draw pie charts to compare these and display them as a poster.

The median

When you have a set of data, it is usual to find its average value. This is useful because it can be used to represent the whole set of data by just a single or typical value.

You have already met one type of average: the mode. This is the value which occurs most often in a set of data. This section explains how to find another type of average: the **median**.

The **median** is the middle value of a set of values when they are put into numerical order.

Example 16.3 Here are the heights of the members of a band:

134 cm   156 cm   161 cm   170 cm   172 cm

The median is the middle number of the set when written in order. This list is already in order of size, so the median is the middle of this list, which is 161 cm.

The median height of the band members is 161 cm.

Example 16.4 Here are the ages of 11 players in a football squad. Find the median of their ages.

23 19 24 26 28 27 24 23 20 23 26

First put the ages in order:

19 20 23 23 23 24 24 26 26 27 28

The median is the number in the middle of the set. So, the median age is 24.

Exercise 16B

1 Find the median of each of these sets of data.

     a   1, 3, 3, 5, 6, 7, 7

     b   11, 12, 13, 13, 14, 14, 15, 15, 16

     c   1, 2, 3, 4, 5, 5, 7

     d   1, 3, 8, 9, 9, 10, 11

     e   21, 21, 23, 25, 29, 31, 32

     f   102, 108, 110, 111, 132

     g   15, 15, 15, 15, 17, 17, 18, 19, 25

     h   42, 42, 53, 62, 79, 79, 82

     i   1003, 1009, 1500, 1781, 1983, 2016, 5132

2 Find the median of each of these sets of data.

     a   8p, 9p, 10p, 15p, 25p

     b   £5, £8, £9, £10, £15, £16, £20

     c   3 cm, 4 cm, 8 cm, 15 cm, 18 cm, 18 cm, 19 cm

     d   100 g, 110 g, 125 g, 150 g, 150 g, 175 g, 215 g

     e   34 km, 45 km, 67 km, 78 km, 88 km, 89 km, 95 km, 109 km, 115 km

     f   57 kg, 58 kg, 58 kg, 61 kg, 63 kg, 67 kg, 71 kg

3 Put the following lists of data into order of size, then find the median of each.

     a   3, 7, 1, 9, 5

     b   11, 83, 54, 28, 12

     c   108, 103, 107, 100, 103, 111, 101

     d   1002, 987, 999, 1002, 1100, 199, 1000

     e   3, 8, 1, 0, 8, 9, 3, 6, 5, 7, 7, 3, 9, 0, 10, 9, 1

     f   33, 39, 38, 32, 30, 37, 31, 35, 38

4 Put the following lists of data into order of size, then find the median of each.

    a £2.50, £1.80, £3.65, £3.80, £4.20, £3.25, £1.80

    b 23 kg, 18 kg, 22 kg, 31 kg, 29 kg, 32 kg, 25 kg

    c 132 cm, 145 cm, 151 cm, 132 cm, 140 cm, 142 cm, 148 cm

    d 32°, 36°, 32°, 30°, 31°, 29°, 31°, 34°, 33°, 32°, 35°

Extension **Work**

Average score

1 Throw a normal dice 11 times. Record your results on a tally chart. What is the median score?

2 Throw a normal dice 21 times. Record your results on a tally chart. What is the median score?

3 Throw a normal dice 51 times. Record your results on a tally chart. What is the median score?

4 Write down anything you notice as you throw the dice more times.

Two way tables

In the media you will often see two way tables that show information.

Example 16.5

Vicky did a survey of the time spent on homework the previous night of all the pupils in her class. This table shows her results.

	Number of boys	Number of girls
Under 1 hour	13	9
1 hour or more	3	5

By reading the individual cells, you can interpret the data as:

- 13 boys spent under 1 hour doing their homework
- 9 girls spent under 1 hour doing their homework
- 3 boys spent 1 hour or more doing their homework
- 5 girls spent 1 hour or more doing their homework

By adding all the cells, you can tell that there were 30 pupils in Vicky's class.

Exercise 16C

1 Adeel did a survey of the eye colour of all the pupils in his class. This table shows his results.

	Number of boys	Number of girls
Blue eyes	9	11
Brown eyes	4	6

    a How many pupils are in Adeel's class?

    b How many boys in Adeel's class have blue eyes?

    c How many girls in Adeel's class have brown eyes?

    d How many pupils in Adeel's class have blue eyes?

    e How many boys are there in Adeel's class?

2 Shauna did a survey of how all the pupils in her class travelled to school. This table shows her results.

	Number of boys	Number of girls
Walked	10	4
Bus	6	9

a How many pupils are in Shauna's class?

b How many boys in Shauna's class walked to school?

c How many girls in Shauna's class travelled by bus?

d How many pupils in Shauna's class walked to school?

e How many girls are there in Shauna's class?

3 Chi did a survey of hair colour of all the pupils in her class. This table shows her results.

	Number of boys	Number of girls
Dark	12	6
Light	4	9

a How many pupils are in Chi's class?

b How many boys in Chi's class had light hair?

c How many girls in Chi's class had dark hair?

d How many pupils in Chi's class had dark hair?

e How many girls are there in Chi's class?

4 Thomas does a survey of cats and dogs as pets of 12 friends in his class. He records his results like this:

Boy or girl	Girl	Girl	Girl	Boy	Girl	Boy	Boy	Girl	Girl	Girl	Girl	Boy
Pets	Dog	Dog	Cat	Dog	Cat	Cat	Dog	Dog	Dog	Cat	Cat	Dog

Copy and complete this table to show Thomas's results.

	Number of boys	Number of girls
Dog		
Cat		

5 There are 17 boys and 12 girls in Padmini's class.

8 boys and 4 girls have dark hair. The others all have light hair.

Copy and complete this table for Padmini's class.

	Number of boys	Number of girls
Dark hair		
Light hair		

Extension Work

Create two way tables for data within your own class. Some examples are given below:

a Brown eyes or blue eyes

b Can swim or cannot swim

c Dark hair or light hair

d Holiday abroad or holiday in Britain

e Can ride a bike or cannot ride a bike

Statistical surveys

You are about to carry out your own statistical survey and write a report on your findings.

Once you have chosen a problem to investigate, you will first need to plan how you intend to carry out the survey and decide how you are going to collect your data.

Your data may be obtained in one of the following ways:

- A survey of a sample of people. Your sample size should be more than 30. To collect data from your chosen sample, you will need to use a data collection sheet or a questionnaire.
- Carrying out experiments. You will need to keep a record of your observations on a data collection sheet.
- Searching other sources. Examples are reference books, newspapers, ICT databases and the Internet.

If you plan to use a data collection sheet, remember the following points:

- Decide what types of data you need to collect.
- Design the layout of your sheet before you start the survey.
- Keep a tally of your results in a table.

If you plan to use a questionnaire, remember the following points:

- Make the questions short and simple.
- Choose questions that require simple responses. For example: Yes, No, Do not know. Or use tick boxes with a set of multichoice answers.
- Avoid personal and embarrassing questions.
- Never ask a leading question designed to get a particular response.

When you have collected all your data, you are ready to write a report on your findings.

Your report should be short and based only on the evidence you have collected. Use averages (the mean, the median or the mode) and the range, to help give an overall picture of the facts. Also, use statistical diagrams to illustrate your results and to make them easier to understand. For example, you can draw bar charts, line graphs or pie charts. Try to give a reason why you have chosen to use a particular type of diagram.

To give your report a more professional look, use ICT software to illustrate the data.

Finally, you will need to write a short conclusion based on your evidence.

Exercise 16D

 Write your own statistical report on one or more of the following problems.

Remember:

- Decide on your sample size.
- Decide whether you need to use a data collection sheet or a questionnaire.
- Find any relevant averages.
- Illustrate your report with suitable diagrams or graphs, and explain why you have used them.
- Write a short conclusion based on all the evidence.

The data can be collected from people in your class or year group, but it may be possible to collect the data from other sources, friends and family outside school.

1 The amount of TV young people watch.

2 The types of sport young people take part in outside school.

3 The musical likes and dislikes of Year 7 pupils.

4 Investigate the young woman's statement: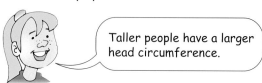

Taller people have a larger head circumference.

5 'More people are taking holidays abroad this year.' Investigate this statement.

Extension Work

Write your own statistical report on one or more of the following problems. For these problems, you will need to use other sources to collect the data.

1 Do football teams in the First Division score more goals than teams in the Second Division?

2 Compare the frequency of letters in the English language to the frequency of letters in the French language.

3 Compare the prices of second-hand cars using different motoring magazines.

LEVEL BOOSTER

4
I can draw simple pie charts.
I can find the median from a list of data.
I can read two way tables.

National Test questions

1 *2007 3–5 Paper 2*

Hedgehogs and dormice are small animals that sleep throughout the winter.

The **shaded** parts of the chart show **when they sleep**.

Use the chart to answer these questions:

a Hedgehogs go to sleep in the middle of November. For **how many months** do they sleep?

b Look at this statement:

Dormice sleep for **more than half of the year**.

Is the statement true? Explain your answer.

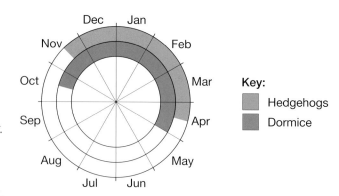

Red kites are large birds that were very rare in England.

Scientists set free some red kites in 1989 and hoped that they would build nests.

The diagrams show how many nests the birds built from 1991 to 1996.

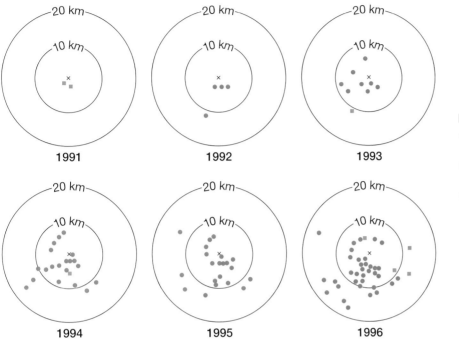

1991   **1992**   **1993**

1994   **1995**   **1996**

Key:

× shows where the birds were set free

▪ represents a nest without eggs

• represents a nest with eggs

Use the diagrams to answer these questions:

a   Which was the first year there were nests **with eggs**?

b   In **1993**, how many nests were **without eggs**?

c   In **1995**, how many nests were **more than 10 km** from where the birds were set free?

d   Explain what happened to the **number** of nests over the years.

e   Now explain what happened to the **distances** of the nests from where the birds were set free, over the years.

This chapter is going to show you

- How to multiply and divide decimals by whole numbers
- How to test for divisibility
- How to find factors
- How to calculate fractions and percentages of quantities

What you should already know

- How to do long and short multiplication and division with whole numbers
- Equivalence of simple fractions, decimals and percentages

Adding and subtracting decimals

You have already met addition and subtraction of decimals in Chapter 2. In this section, you will be doing problems involving whole numbers, decimals and metric units.

Example 17.1 Work out: **a** $4 + 0.8 + 0.7$ **b** $6 - 1.4$

a A whole number has a decimal point after the units digit. So, put in zeros for the missing place values, and line up the decimal points:

$$
\begin{array}{r}
4.0 \\
0.8 \\
+\,0.7 \\
\hline
5.5 \\
\end{array}
$$
    1

b As in the previous sum, put in zeros to make up the missing place values, and line up the decimal points:

$$
\begin{array}{r}
^{5\;\;1}\!\!\!\!\not{6}.0 \\
-\,1.4 \\
\hline
4.6 \\
\end{array}
$$

Example 17.2 Nazia has done 4.3 km of a 20 km bike ride. How far does Nazia still have to go?

The units are the same, so:

$$
\begin{array}{r}
^{1\;9\;1}\!\!\!\!2\not{0}.0 \\
-\;\;4.3 \\
\hline
15.7 \\
\end{array}
$$

Nazia still has 15.7 km to go.

Example 17.3

Mary wants to lose 3 kg in weight. So far she has lost 600 grams. How much more does she need to lose?

The units need to be made the same. So change 600 grams into 0.6 kg. This gives:

$$\begin{array}{r} {}^{2}\,{}^{1}\\ \not{3}.0 \\ -\ 0.6 \\ \hline 2.4 \end{array}$$

Mary still has to lose 2.4 kg.

Exercise 17A

1 Without using a calculator, work out each of these.

a	3.5 + 4.7	**b**	6.1 + 2.8	**c**	3.4 + 1. 7
d	12.41 + 8.69	**e**	9.3 – 6.1	**f**	3.5 – 2.7
g	17.5 – 13.7	**h**	27.65 – 16.47		

2 Without using a calculator, work out each of these.

a	3.2 + 1.2	**b**	2.5 + 1.3	**c**	2.7 + 1.4	**d**	2.4 + 1.2
e	52.1 + 23.2 + 0.9						

3 Without using a calculator, work out each of these.

a	4 – 2.3	**b**	5 – 1.2	**c**	8 – 3.1	**d**	12 – 2.3
e	7 – 1.8	**f**	10 – 2.6	**g**	24 – 12.3	**h**	15 – 6.1

4 The three legs of a relay are 3 km, 4.8 km and 1.8 km. How far is the race altogether?

Extension Work

Write down all the pairs of single-digit numbers that add up to 9: for example, 2 + 7.

By looking at your answers to Question 3 in Exercise 17A and working out the following:

a 1 – 0.4   **b** 6 – 2.5   **c** 12 – 3.6

explain how you can just write down the answers when you are taking away a decimal from a whole number.

Make a poster to explain this to a Year 6 student.

Multiplying and dividing decimals

When you add together 1.2 + 1.2 + 1.2 + 1.2, you get 4.8.

This sum can be written as 4 × 1.2 = 4.8. It can also be written as 4.8 ÷ 4 = 1.2.

You are now going to look at how to multiply and divide decimals by whole numbers.

These two operations are just like any type of multiplication and division but you need to be sure where to put the decimal point. As a general rule, there will be the same number of decimal places in the answer as there were in the original problem.

Example 17.4 ▷ Work out: **a** 5×3.7 **b** 8×4.3 **c** 9×1.8 **d** 6×3.5

Each of these can be set out in a column:

a
$$\begin{array}{r} 3.7 \\ \times\ \ 5 \\ \hline 18.5 \\ {\scriptstyle 3} \end{array}$$

b
$$\begin{array}{r} 4.3 \\ \times\ \ 8 \\ \hline 34.4 \\ {\scriptstyle 2} \end{array}$$

c
$$\begin{array}{r} 1.8 \\ \times\ \ 9 \\ \hline 16.2 \\ {\scriptstyle 7} \end{array}$$

d
$$\begin{array}{r} 3.5 \\ \times\ \ 6 \\ \hline 21.0 \\ {\scriptstyle 3} \end{array}$$

See how the decimal point stays in the *same* place. You would give the answer to part **d** as 21.

Example 17.5 ▷ Work out: **a** $22.8 \div 6$ **b** $33.6 \div 7$ **c** $9.8 \div 7$

Each of these can be set out as short division:

a
$$6\overline{)22.8^{4}}\quad 3.8$$

b
$$7\overline{)33.6^{5}}\quad 4.8$$

c
$$7\overline{)9.8^{2}}\quad 1.4$$

Once again, the decimal point stays in the same place.

4
5

Exercise 17B

1 Without using a calculator, work out each of these.

   a 31×5 **b** 17×8 **c** 14×6 **d** 22×9

   e 6×33 **f** 9×56 **g** 5×61 **h** 9×91

2 Without using a calculator, work out each of these.

   a 3.1×5 **b** 1.7×8 **c** 1.4×6 **d** 2.2×9

   e 6×3.3 **f** 9×5.6 **g** 5×6.1 **h** 9×9.1

3 Without using a calculator, work out each of these.

   a $176 \div 8$ **b** $392 \div 7$ **c** $272 \div 8$

   d $305 \div 5$ **e** $256 \div 4$ **f** $42 \div 3$

   g $279 \div 9$ **h** $225 \div 5$

4 Without using a calculator, work out each of these.

   a $17.6 \div 8$ **b** $39.2 \div 7$ **c** $27.2 \div 8$ **d** $30.5 \div 5$

   e $25.6 \div 4$ **f** $4.2 \div 3$ **g** $27.9 \div 9$ **h** $22.5 \div 5$

FM 5 A plank of wood, 2.8 metres long, is cut into four equal pieces. How long is each piece?

FM 6 A cake weighing 1.8 kg is cut into three equal pieces. How much does each piece weigh?

Use a calculator to work out each of the following.

a 46×3 **b** 4.6×3 **c** 4.6×0.3 **d** 0.46×0.3

Try some examples of your own.

You will notice that the digits of all the answers are the same but that the decimal point is in different places. Can you see the rule for placing the decimal point?

Divisibility and multiples

You should be able to recall these number facts:

- Numbers that are divisible by 2 end in 0, 2, 4, 6 or 8.
- Numbers that are divisible by 3 have digits that add up to multiples of 3.
- Numbers that are divisible by 5 end in 5 or 0.
- Numbers that are divisible by 10 end in 0.

Example 17.6

Draw a table for the numbers 12, 15, 20, 38, 45 and 120 which shows whether they are divisible by 2, 3, 5 and 10.

Number	Divisible by 2	Divisible by 3	Divisible by 5	Divisible by 10
12	Yes	Yes	No	No
15	No	Yes	Yes	No
20	Yes	No	Yes	Yes
38	Yes	No	No	No
45	No	Yes	Yes	No
120	Yes	Yes	Yes	Yes

Example 17.7

Write down each of these.
a The multiples of 7 between 20 and 40. **b** The multiples of 8 between 10 and 50.

a 21 28 35
These are the numbers in the 7 times table between 20 and 40.

b 16 24 32 40 48
These are the numbers in the 8 times table between 10 and 50.

Example 17.8

Give an example to show that each of the following statements is false.

a Multiples of 3 are always odd. **b** Multiples of 6 are also multiples of 4.

a The multiples of 3 are 3, 6, 9, 12, 15, …., where 6 and 12 are even. These are called **counter examples**.

b The multiples of 6 are 6, 12, 18, 24, 30, …, where 6, 18, and 30 are not multiples of 4.

Exercise 17C

1 Write down all the multiples of 5 between 13 and 51.

2 Write down all the multiples of 2 between 9 and 21.

3 Write down all the multiples of 3 between 17 and 37.

4 Write down all the multiples of 6 between 10 and 40.

5 Write down the three numbers below that are multiples of 3 *and* multiples of 4.

48   36   30   34   75   21   60

6 Copy and complete this table.

Number	Divisible by 2	Divisible by 10	Divisible by 5	Divisible by 4
45	No	No	Yes	No
70				
24				
47				
125				
160				

7 Say whether each of the following statements is true or false. If it is false, give an example that shows it.

a All multiples of 4 are even.

b All multiples of 5 are odd.

c All multiples of 9 less than 90 have digits that add up to 9.

d All multiples of 10 are also multiples of 5.

e All multiples of 3 are also multiples of 6.

Extension **Work**

1 Write down numbers that are multiples of both 3 *and* 4.

2 Write down numbers that are multiples of both 3 *and* 5.

3 Write down numbers that are multiples of both 2 *and* 5.

4 Can you see a rule that connects the numbers?

5 Does your rule work for numbers that are:

a Multiples of both 2 *and* 10 at the same time?

b Multiples of both 3 *and* 9 at the same time?

Factors of numbers

A factor is a number that divides exactly into another number.

Example 17.9 Draw a factor diagram for: **a** 14   **b** 12

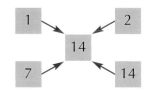

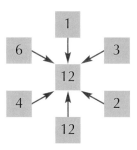

Example 17.10 Find the factors of: **a** 18   **b** 25   **c** 17

a Find all the products that make 18:
$1 \times 18 = 18$ $2 \times 9 = 18$ $3 \times 6 = 18$
So, the factors of 18 are {1, 2, 3, 6, 9, 18}.

b $1 \times 25 = 25$ $5 \times 5 = 25$
5 is repeated but only written down once.
So, the factors of 25 are {1, 5, 25}.

c $1 \times 17 = 17$
The factors of 17 are {1, 17}. 17 is a **prime number**.

Example 17.11 Write down the first five prime numbers.

There is no pattern to the prime numbers, so you have to learn them. The first 5 are:
2 3 5 7 11

Exercise 17D

1 Copy and complete the factor diagram for: **a**   8   **b**   21

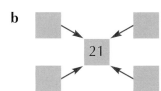

2 9 has three factors. Write down the factors of 9.

3 32 has six factors. Write down the factors of 32.

4 Find the factors of each of these.
a   10   **b**   20   **c**   30   **d**   40   **e**   50

5 Find the factors of each of these.

   a 6   **b** 16   **c** 24   **d** 26   **e** 28

   f 36   **g** 48

6 Write down the first ten prime numbers.

Extension Work

Write down the numbers from 1 to 48 in a grid that is six numbers wide. Shade all the numbers that are **not** prime numbers.

The unshaded numbers are the prime numbers below 50. You should try to learn them.

1	2	3	4	5	6
7	8	9	10	11	12
13	14	15			

Percentages of quantities

This section will show you how to calculate simple percentages of quantities. This section will also revise the equivalence between fractions, percentages and decimals.

Example 17.12

Calculate: **a** 15% of £600   **b** 40% of £30

Calculate 10%, then use multiples of this.

a 10% of £600 = £60, 5% = £30. So, 15% of £600 = 60 + 30 = £90.

b 10% of £30 = £3. So, 40% of £30 = 4 × 3 = £12.

Example 17.13

Write down the equivalent percentage and fraction for each of these decimals.

a 0.6   **b** 0.25

To change a decimal to a percentage, multiply by 100. This gives:

a 60%   **b** 25%

To change a decimal to a fraction, divide by 10, 100, 1000 as appropriate and cancel if possible. This gives:

a $0.6 = \frac{6}{10} = \frac{3}{5}$ **b** $0.25 = \frac{25}{100} = \frac{1}{4}$

Example 17.14

Write down the equivalent percentage and decimal for each of these fractions.

a $\frac{7}{10}$ **b** $\frac{3}{5}$

To change a fraction into a percentage, make the denominator 100. This gives:

a $\frac{7}{10} = \frac{70}{100} = 70\%$ **b** $\frac{3}{5} = \frac{60}{100} = 60\%$

To change a fraction into a decimal, divide the top by the bottom, or make into a percentage, then divide by 100. This gives:

a 0.7   **b** 0.6

Example 17.15

Write down the equivalent decimal and fraction for each of these percentages.

a 90%　　　　　　　**b** 20%

To change a percentage to a decimal, divide by 100. This gives: **a** 0.9　　**b** 0.2

To change a percentage to a fraction, make a fraction over 100 then cancel if possible. This gives:

a $90\% = \frac{90}{100} = \frac{9}{10}$　　**b** $20\% = \frac{20}{100} = \frac{1}{5}$

Exercise 17E

1 Calculate each of these.

a 35% of £300　　**b** 15% of £200　　**c** 60% of £20　　**d** 20% of £140
e 45% of £400　　**f** 5% of £40　　**g** 40% of £50　　**h** 25% of £24

2 A bus garage holds 50 buses. They are either single-deckers or double-deckers. 30% are single deckers.

a How many single-deckers are there?
b How many double-deckers are there?
c What percentage are double-deckers?

3 Copy and complete this table by working out the equivalent decimals, fractions and percentages.

Decimal	0.1		0.4			0.8	1.0
Fraction	$\frac{1}{10}$	$\frac{1}{5}$		$\frac{1}{2}$	$\frac{7}{10}$		
Percentage	10%	30%		60%		90%	

4 Write down each of these fractions as both a percentage and a decimal.

a $\frac{1}{4}$　　**b** $\frac{3}{4}$　　**c** $\frac{1}{3}$　　**d** $\frac{2}{3}$

Extension Work

Copy the cross-number puzzle. Use the clues to fill it in. Then use the completed puzzle to fill in the missing numbers in the clues.

Across
1　70% of 300
3　75% of 200
5　75% of 700
8　25% of ......
9　80% of 400

Down
1　50% of ......
2　21% of ......
3　50% of 24
4　25% of 600
6　25% of 1000
7　75% of 44

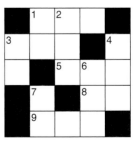

Solving problems

Below are some real-life problems. Before you start, read each question carefully and think about the mathematics you are going to use. Show your working clearly. You may find the multiplication grid you did at the start of the last maths lesson helpful.

5

Exercise 17F

1 Packets of Super Mints hold 6 mint sweets. Mr Smith buys a box of 144 packets of Super Mints. How many individual mints does he have?

2 As a special offer, the sweet company are giving 7 mints in a packet. Mr Jones has 135 special packets. How many more mints has Mr Jones got than Mr Smith?

FM 3 Flights to Florida are £362. How much will five flights cost?

FM 4 To measure the width of a corridor, Melanie paces out the width using her shoes. The corridor is 7 shoe lengths wide. One shoe length is 18 cm. How wide is the corridor?

FM 5 To measure the length of the corridor, Sarfraz uses a scrap piece of wood. The corridor is 9 wood lengths long. The piece of wood is 1.8 metres long. How long is the corridor?

6 Using only the digits 1, 3, 4, make six different multiplication problems using the boxes below.

☐ ☐ ☐ × 5 =

Work out the answer for each problem.

7 Make six different multiplications using only the digits 2, 3, 4.

☐ × ☐ ☐ =

FM 8 There are 32 digestive biscuits in a packet. If John has 8 packets, will he have enough for 112 people to have 2 biscuits each?

FM 9 The digestive biscuits cost 39p a packet. How much do 8 packets cost?

FM 10 Ahmed buys 5 bags of crisps at 32p each. How much change does he get from a £5 note?

LEVEL BOOSTER

3 I can solve simple whole number problems involving multiplication and division.

4 I can use simple fractions and percentages to describe proportions of a whole.
I can add and subtract decimals to two places.
I can multiply and divide using whole numbers.

1 *2007 3–5 Paper 1*

Here is part of the 36 times table.

Use the 36 times table to help you work out the missing numbers.

288 ÷ 8 = ☐   180 ÷ 36 = ☐   11 × 36 = ☐

```
 1 × 36 =  36
 2 × 36 =  72
 3 × 36 = 108
 4 × 36 = 144
 5 × 36 = 180
 6 × 36 = 216
 7 × 36 = 252
 8 × 36 = 288
 9 × 36 = 324
10 × 36 = 360
```

 2 *2005 3–5*

In a theatre, tickets are three different prices.

Ticket in seating area **A**   £19.00
Ticket in seating area **B**   £29.00
Ticket in seating area **C**   £39.00

a How many tickets in area **A** can you buy with £100?

b How many tickets in area **B** can you buy with £200?

c Jo buys **two** tickets in area **C**.
She pays with **two £50 notes**.

How much change should she get?

3 *2006 4–6 Paper 1*

a Add together 1740 and 282.

b Now **add** together 17.4 and 2.82.
You can use part **a** to help you.

c 3.5 + 2.35 is **bigger** than 3.3 + 2.1.

How much bigger?

4 *2006 4–6 Paper 1*

a Add together **3.7** and **6.5**.

b Subtract **5.7** from **15.2**.

c Multiply **254** by **5**.

d Divide **342** by **6**.

FM Running a small business – a group activity

Plan

1 You are setting up a small business to buy materials, make gadgets and sell them for profit.

Facts

2 You have £20 000 to invest in your business.

One machine to produce your gadgets costs £2000.

The machines also cost £1000 per week each to maintain.

Each machine can produce 100 gadgets per day but requires two workers to use it.

Workers are paid £500 per week each.

The cost of materials to produce one gadget is £10.

Weekly sales figures

3 The number of sales depends on the selling price. The table shows maximum weekly sales for different selling prices.

Selling price	£18	£19	£20
Maximum number of gadgets that can be sold per week	3000	2000	1000

Your aim

4 To make as much profit as possible at the end of 6 weeks.

Hints and tactics

5 Try buying different numbers of machines to start with.

Use some of your profits to buy extra machines.

Sell at the highest of the three selling prices that you can.

Your **total costs** cannot be greater than the amount of money you have at the start of any week.

An example

6 Here is an example of a week if you buy one machine and employ two workers.

Be careful: If you buy four machines you cannot pay any workers to produce gadgets and will be bankrupt!

Week 1
(£20 000 available to spend)

Cost of machines bought	$1 \times £2000 = £2000$		Income = Selling price × Number of gadgets sold	$£25 \times 500 = £12\,500$
Maintenance cost of machines	$1 \times £1000 = £1000$			
Cost of workers	$2 \times £500 = £1000$		Total profit	$£12\,500 - £9000 = £3500$
Number of gadgets produced	500			
Cost of materials	$500 \times £10 = £5000$			
Total costs	£9000		Balance	$£20\,000 + £3500 = £23\,500$

Profit for week 1 = £3500
Amount available to spend in week 2 = £23 500

<table>
<tr><td>

This chapter is going to show you

- The names and properties of polygons
- How to tessellate 2-D shapes
- How to make 3-D models

</td><td>

What you should already know

- How to reflect, rotate and translate shapes
- How to draw and measure angles
- How to calculate the angles on a straight line and around a point
- How to draw nets for 3-D shapes

</td></tr>
</table>

Polygons

A **polygon** is any 2-D shape that has straight sides.

The names of the most common polygons are given in the table below.

Number of sides	Name of polygon
3	Triangle
4	Quadrilateral
5	Pentagon
6	Hexagon
7	Heptagon
8	Octagon
9	Nonagon
10	Decagon

A **convex polygon** is one with all its diagonals inside the polygon.

A **concave polygon** is one with at least one diagonal outside the polygon.

Example 18.1

A convex pentagon
(all diagonals inside)

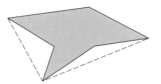

A concave hexagon
(two diagonals outside)

A **regular polygon** has all its sides equal and all its interior angles equal.

Example 18.2 A regular octagon has eight lines of symmetry and rotational symmetry of order 8.

Exercise 18A

1 Which shapes below are polygons? If they are, write down their names.

a 　　b 　　c

d 　　e

2 Which shapes below are regular polygons?

a 　　b 　　c

d 　　e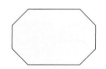

3 State whether each of the shapes below is a convex polygon or a concave polygon.

a 　　b 　　c

d 　　e

4 Try to draw a pentagon which has:

   a one interior right angle.　　 **b** two interior right angles.

   c three interior right angles.　　**d** four interior right angles.

5 Draw hexagons which have exactly:

   a no lines of symmetry.　　 **b** one line of symmetry.

   c two lines of symmetry.　　 **d** three lines of symmetry.

Extension **Work**

1 How to construct a regular hexagon.

a Draw a circle of radius 5 cm.

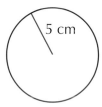

5 cm

b With your compasses still set to a radius of 5 cm, go round the circumference of the circle making marks 5 cm apart.

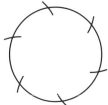

c Use a ruler to join the points where the marks cross the circle.

2 A triangle has no diagonals. A quadrilateral has two diagonals.

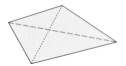

How many diagonals can you draw inside a pentagon and a hexagon? Copy and complete the table below.

Name of polygon	Number of sides	Number of diagonals
Triangle	3	0
Quadrilateral	4	2
Pentagon	5	…
Hexagon	6	…
……	7	…
……	8	…

Tessellations

A **tessellation** is a pattern made by fitting together the same shapes without leaving any gaps. When drawing a tessellation, use a square or a triangular grid, as in the examples below. To show a tessellation, it is usual to draw up to about ten repeating shapes.

Example **18.3**

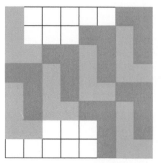

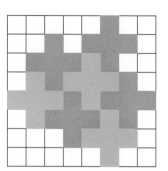

Two different shapes which each makes a tessellation on a square grid.

Example 18.4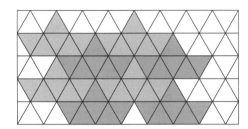

This shape tessellates on a triangular grid.

Example 18.5

Circles *do not* tessellate.

However you try to fit circles together, there will always be gaps.

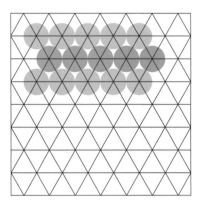

Exercise 18B

1 Make a tessellation for each of the following shapes. Use a square grid.

a  b   c   d

2 Make a tessellation for each of the following shapes. Use a triangular grid.

a   b   c   d

Extension **Work**

1 Design a tessellation of your own. Working in pairs or groups, make an attractive poster to show all your different tessellations.

2 Here is a tessellation which uses curves. Can you design a different curved tessellation?

Constructing 3-D shapes

A net is a 2-D shape which can be cut out and folded up to make a 3-D shape.

To make the nets below into 3-D shapes you will need the following equipment: a sharp pencil, a ruler, a protractor, a pair of scissors and a glue-stick or sticky tape.

Always score the card along the fold-lines using scissors and a ruler. This makes the card much easier to fold properly.

You can glue the edges together using the tabs or you can just use sticky tape. If you decide to use glue, then always keep one face of the shape free of tabs and glue down this face last.

Example 18.6 **Constructing a square-based pyramid**

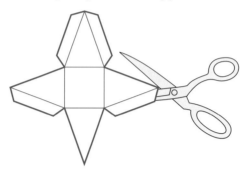 

1 Carefully cut out the net using scissors.   **2** Score along each fold-line using a ruler and scissors.

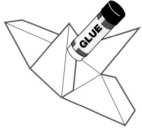 

3 Fold along each fold-line and stick the shape together by gluing each tab.   **4** The last face to stick down is the one without any tabs.

Exercise 18C Draw each of the following nets accurately on card. Cut out the net and construct the 3-D shape.

1 **A cube**

 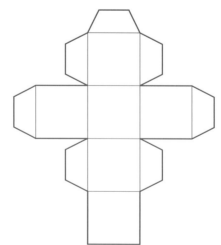

Each square has side 4 cm.

4 cm

4 cm

2 A cuboid

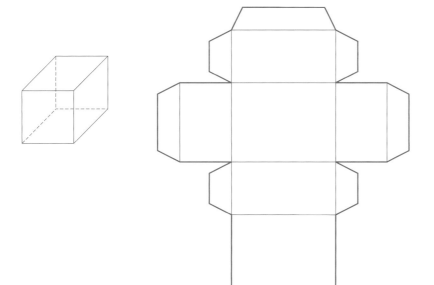

The rectangles have the following measurements.

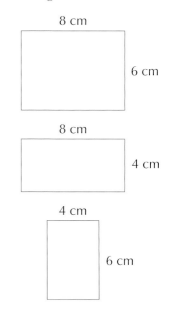

8 cm

6 cm

8 cm

4 cm

4 cm

6 cm

3 Regular tetrahedron

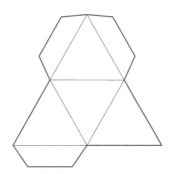

Each equilateral triangle has these measurements:

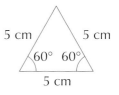

5 cm   5 cm
60° 60°
5 cm

4 Triangular prism

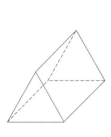

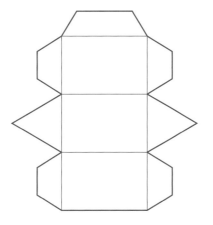

Each rectangle has these measurements:

6 cm

4 cm

Each equilateral triangle has these measurements:

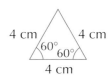

4 cm   4 cm
60° 60°
4 cm

Extension **Work**

The following nets are for more complex 3-D shapes. Choose suitable measurements and make each shape from card. The tabs have not been included for you.

1 Octahedron

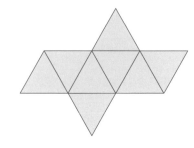

2 Regular hexagonal prism

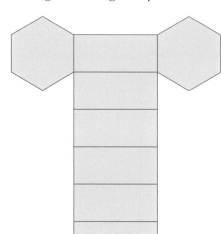

3 Truncated square-based pyramid

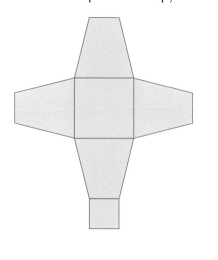

LEVEL BOOSTER

  I know the names of and how to draw common polygons.

  I know how to tessellate 2-D shapes.
I can make 3-D models from a net.

3

1 *2003 3–5 Paper 2*

    a Look at these shapes.

        Explain why they are **hexagons**.

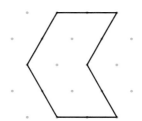  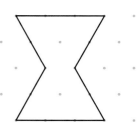

Isometric grid

    b On a copy of a grid like the one below, draw a **regular hexagon**.

Isometric grid

4

2 *2006 3–5 Paper 2*

I use two congruent trapeziums to make the shapes below.

Which of these shapes are **hexagons**?

  a   **b**   **c**   **d**

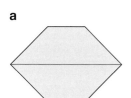  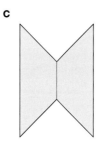 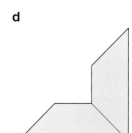

3 *2000 Paper 1*

The sketch shows the net of a triangular prism.

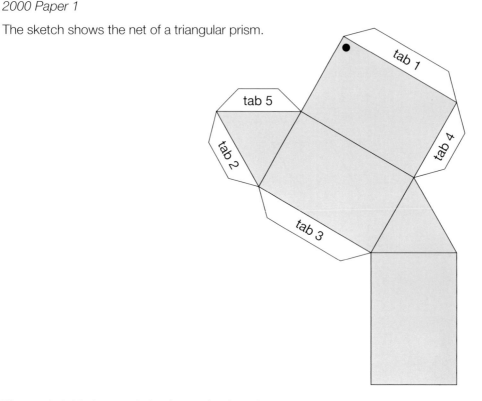

The net is folded up and glued to make the prism.

a Which edge is tab 1 glued to? On a copy of the diagram, label this edge A.

b Which edge is tab 2 glued to? Label this edge B.

c The corner marked ● meets two other corners. Label these two other corners ●.

4 *2001 Paper 1*

The diagram shows a box. Draw the net for the box on a square grid.

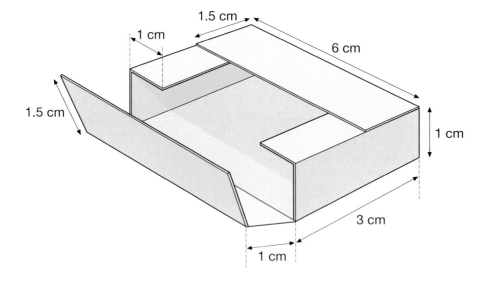

Index